WITH THESE HANDS

A COUNTRY GIRL CAME TO TOWN

Bonnie Taylor-Williams

D1295592

Published by Bonnie Taylor-Williams, Inc.
Copyright © 2015 by Bonnie Taylor-Williams

ISBN: 978-0-9908203-0-7 (Trade Print)
ISBN: 978-0-9908203-2-1 (Hard Cover)
ISBN: 978-0-9908203-1-4 (eBook)

Content/Copy Editor: Dr. Maxine Thompson
Cover designed by Marion Designs

Disclaimer: Some names and details have been changed and/or omitted to protect the privacy of individuals.

DEDICATION

$\mathcal{I}$ dedicate this book to my missing links; my Uncle El, "Ain't It Funky Now," "Fair For A Square," "Chicken Lickin'" "Love" Hair Weev Master; my "Granny," Love You. If you needed it, Granny had it; Granny Mary Green. My favorite cousin Paulette Green who became the best Aunt I ever had, my favorite chef, and though she was a nurse, the best family doctor; my grandfather, Elmer, my father, Herbert Taylor, for helping, teaching and nurturing me, and my Uncle Paul, another one of the family's entrepreneurs.

It's also dedicated to Donald Carroway, Lester Woodhouse, Mikki Kelly, Louvenia Wilkes, Juanita Garmen, Ermalene Dillard, and Orville Nelson.

ACKNOWLEDGMENTS

I acknowledge God, without HIM nothing is possible, with HIM everything is possible.

I acknowledge my grandmother, Selena, who learned and taught a trade. She also taught the importance of hard work, professionalism, kindness and strength that enabled more than three generations with skills to live a good life, never wanting for anything. I thank her for living her life in such a way that not only made me want to share her story, but it sparked an interest in many others over the years who went from asking her to write a book to encouraging me to write it

My mother, Juanita, the best mother in the world to me and for me, for sharing her love for reading with my brothers and me; by sitting us down at the kitchen table, teaching us how to spell, sound out and define words before creating sentences. My mother opened our minds further by walking us to the public library and applying for a library card for each one of us, which ignited my love for reading and writing. I thank her for being smart enough to be obedient by learning from "mistakes" and listening to her mother, enabling her to train my brothers and me in the way we should travel this map of life, which she led us with love, respect and obedience. As a young mother with the help of my grandmother, my great grandmother, my uncle and aunt she instilled the importance of family and learning the family business of Beauty and the art of Hair Weev technology before starting her own transportation business and serving the schools of the city of Chicago.

To my husband, Paxton, for years of love, faith and encouragement, to my brothers, Bryant T and Herbert "Scotty," who share my "storytelling" memories and their many loving words of encouragement and harassment. To my father, Eddie Dunbar, the hardest working man I know, who helped instill in me everything is possible if you're willing to work for it. To my niece, Chante', who encouraged me with gifts of other books of family history, my cousins Jasmine and Chastity, family, friends and clients, especially Vernissia, Evelyn and Donna who never stopped believing in me.

I would like to thank all of my coaches (past and present), Kinora Maxwell, my editor, Dr. Maxine Thompson, my photographer Essential Photography, my book cover designer, Marion Designs, my website developer Modernday Hippie. To Gwendetta Albright, Senator Carol Mosley Braun, Ernest Daurahm, Herb Kent, Brenda Daurahm, Natalie Haskell, Katherine, Arlene Ward, Jan Vernie, Bria, Holle Thee Maxwell and Ella Curry. To the many, many clients that patronized Selena's House of Beauty. To anyone who has encouraged me, taught me anything, shared knowledge, wisdom or friendship, loved me and prayed for me I thank and acknowledge ALL OF YOU!

As much as I am grateful for the past I acknowledge the future; anyone who has a dream beginning with my nieces and nephews, Ceasar, Brandon, Brittany, Jonathan, Lovell, Eric, Krishaun, Donald, Jonathan, Janae', Jacobe, Jada, Elijah, Mia, Ajae, Jacob, Bridgette and Jamal; anyone who in spite of any mistakes or mishaps feel that it's too late, or that they're at the bottom.

IF YOU'RE ABOVE GROUND YOU'RE ON TOP! IF YOU CAN LOOK UP YOU CAN GET UP...KEEP GETTING UP!!!

QUOTES OF ADMIRATION

Selena Parker as I knew her back in the day.... The 1940s on the west side of Chicago in the Robert Brooks projects, to be exact on 14thStreet between Throop and Loomis Streets. I remember her in many ways... She could do hair; she could drive, and wow she could really dress up! She also had a "strut" that no one else around our house had.

Almost all of the girls in our front and back rows would go to Selena to get their hair done right in her back pantry room. It was set up as a beauty shop. Selena treated me as if I was one of her own daughters. Juanita and I were the closet. I remember riding with her children in her car, I really cherished those days. I like the respect she had for her Mother and Father who lived separately but very close to us in the same projects. I was so disappointed when she moved away to the Southside of Chicago. That meant all of us, Juanita; me, etc. would not be able to be together. Things were changing all the time as we got older and seeing each other less and less. Now we get to be together at special occasions – weddings, birthdays, retirement parties etc. I will never forget Selena and I thank the Lord for our families knowing each other. By the way it was Selena who encouraged my mother, Marie Henry to become a beautician too.

—Gwendetta Henry Albright

"Selena is not only the baddest chick to pick up a curling iron, but she was a legend when I got started in the business. Selena was so bad, she gave classes on hair weaving, teaching other stylists how to get wealthy in the salons. Selena was driving Classic Tiffanies, Eldorados, Sevilles and Broughams when other stylists were just wishing they could. I became familiar with her when my sister, Brenda, worked for her and she inspired me to accomplish the things that I achieved in the beauty industry and it's no wonder that we're both born under the same sign. It's high time that someone honored her for the contributions that she's made to this business and no one deserves it more."

—Ernest "Ernie" Daurham

"I lived in the Chatham neighborhood as a teenager. Miss Selena's shop on 83rd street was a hub for business in the community, and I remember thinking of her as a modern day "Madame CJ Walker". She pioneered techniques in the beauty industry, and was very influential as an African American entrepreneur. She was a role model for me and many other young women because she was able to overcome barriers created not only by race, but by gender as well. It is a wonderful thing that your book will tell the story of her fearlessness and determination and most of all, her work ethic. Stories like this will help light the way for future generations."

—Senator Carol Moseley Braun

"Knowing Ms. Selena is such an honor and a privilege. Here are a few words I use to describe Ms. Selena; amazing, beautiful, consistent, caring, fabulous and extraordinary and the list goes on. While attending Pivot Point Beauty School in Chicago I met Selena's granddaughter, Bonnie and Selena's son, El. As graduation time was approaching and because we all became very close Bonnie offered me a job at her grandmother's salon, in the Loop, downtown in the Stephens building. After introducing me to Ms. Selena, I was given my first professional salon job....I was so happy and proud. I've always referred to Selena as my God grandmother; she's been a mentor, role model and a positive black business woman. A diva for sure, you go Selena!!!"

—*Love you, Arlene Ward*

"Selena, a lifetime friend, we traveled the world together selling cosmetics and hair; I remember the time Selena and I were overseas selling hair and cosmetics and one lady came over to the Villa where we were staying in the Caribbean and bought $3,000 worth of hair and cosmetics. Selena said "Make sure you get that cash American money" the only woman I know that is about the cash, making money and enjoying her life to the fullest. I Love you, Selena."

—*Katherine*

"One afternoon in 1968, I walked into a fabulous Beauty salon. It was Selena's House of Beauty. Selena was a beautiful, talented black woman who knew how to operate a successful business. I worked in both her Southside and Chicago Loop locations, she was great to work for and to this day I still count it a blessing to have worked for her and to have considered her children and grandchildren as my family too."

—Brenda Daurham,
D'orum Hair Product, 2014

"Oh, I have many memories about Selena's; it was across the street from the Tivoli (Theatre). I had many girlfriends who had their hair done at Selena's House of Beauty! Back in the day black beauticians had reputations akin to singers and boxers today and that's why you went to their shops. Some of these beauticians had really big names and were crowded because of their name and the quality of their work. Selena's of course was rated among the best!"

—Herb Kent the Cool Gent, H. K. the DJ,
Herbie Baby (Chicago's own Legendary DJ) V103

"I met Selena, a nice, pretty brown skin woman, who was always glamourous, well dressed with confidence in the late 1950's. At a time when brown skin and pretty were rarely mentioned in the same sentence; she made me feel I, a brown skin woman, too, could be pretty."

—Phyliss

"SELENA: A LEGEND IN THE HAIR CARE INDUSTRY
Most of the time we think of institutions as buildings, non-personal inanimate objects.

Selena represents the best of the personal side of an institution.

Selena had a vision. She created her business at a time when few women entrepreneurs were attempting to carve out their business. She knew what she wanted. She moved the obstacles out of her way to get there.

Selena's innovations to her craft were a first and she continued to innovate year after year.

She remains an innovator in her industry."

—Jan V. Knight

S E L E N A:

A CLASS ACT
A *SOPHISTICATED *ELEGANT *LEADER,
*EXQUISITELY *NOTED for her *AMBITION

I am Blessed as well as privileged to call her Mother.

*S E L E N A

MY MOTHER…A CLASSY LADY!

—Juanita

TABLE OF CONTENTS

Prologue

On a sweltering summer night in 1957, a live band rocked the house as they performed a soul-stirring Blues show, and was headlined by an up-and-coming blues star who was playing his guitar on the stage. However, when my grandmother, Selena, sashayed into the club, the music stopped. Without a doubt, she took the stage presence over from the back of the room.

Mesmerized, the bluesman stopped strumming his guitar in mid-note. "Get the pretty lady a seat and bring it right down front for me," he instructed one of his paid employees.

Although he tried to continue his song, the bluesman was so enchanted with the young woman's walk that he held the same key on his guitar until his valet retrieved a chair and escorted her and the chair down front. After Selena assured him that she was comfortable and the waitress had delivered her drink of choice, which was a glass of orange juice, (hey, maybe that's why people still ask her to this day… "Where is the fountain of youth?"), the guitar player finally released the chord he was playing. For the rest of the night, he played his signature "down home" blues.

Needless to say, it was kismet that Selena happened to be at the same club where B.B. King was performing. There was something magical about this chance meeting.

That night was what would become the beginning of a long and dear friendship that has spanned over fifty years.

Who knew Selena would become known as the "Queen Of Hair Weev?" Or that Riley, the "Blues Boy" King, would become known as B.B. King, the "King of the Blues?" The two had one thing in common. Both started out with great dreams and big aspirations. They never wanted to pick cotton for a living as their parents had done before them, yet they did not want to starve either, because they chose to follow in different footsteps.

When it was all said and done, I think both of their dreams served them well.

Although each one's dream took them on completely different paths, they both have left their mark on the world. I'll tell you more about them later.

Chapter One

"God's Amazing Grace" is the only explanation for an African American woman in her early thirties, recently divorced from her husband of fifteen years, mother of three young children, and a new business owner of her own beauty salon, all to be described in the same sentence back in the mid-fifties. This was truly an oxymoron. But, from the time my grandmother, Selena, was a young woman, she had chutzpah.

Selena had arrived in Chicago, Illinois, from Memphis, Tennessee, just about sixteen years before she met B.B. King. At the time, she was a teen bride and a brand new mother with a baby girl who was a few months old.

When she first set foot in Chicago, all that Selena owned was in her arms; her baby cradled in one arm and her suitcase, accompanied by her handmade quilt tied to it that her great-aunt had made for her, in the other arm. Selena's young new husband, Elmer, had sent for her and the baby as soon as he got a job.

First, you must know this about my grandmother. Selena was, and still is, a beautiful lady. Her shape was notorious and legendary. Whether she was emptying the garbage or hanging out the family laundry on clothes lines in the Westside projects in Chicago, where she once lived, Selena's figure could insight a parade.

In the early 1940s, Selena was a young housewife, a stay-at-home mom, and an older sister who helped her mother rear her two younger sisters. Back then, her audience consisted of family and neighbors.

Some were nosey, some were pleasant; others were kind and full of advice; but, at the same time, there were those few who spread malice and gossip and who were full of deceit. Many of them admired her, although some of them never told her until decades later. I guess the cold harshness of this world can make you reflect on a kind spirit if you ever experienced one.

Some years later, as Selena's audience grew larger, when she would drive up in front of her beauty shop with her long ponytail blowing in the wind of her 1956 black-and-white hard top convertible Ford, men studied her. She personified a living dream, in that she drove a beautiful car, and was a gorgeous woman shaped like a coca cola bottle to boot. She was everything a man wanted. So statuesque, any description of beauty, elegance, and style that you could imagine was used to describe Selena. She had an impeccable sense of fashion. Men would come out of all the businesses on both sides of the street just to see her and what she was wearing that day. She was sexy enough to make a man have a wet dream in broad daylight.

Mainly, they loved her walk; how her tiny waist perfectly fitted above her voluptuous hips, which curvaceously melted into her pretty legs. This was enough for a man to get a hard on. When any man would scan up to her face and see her pretty smile, he witnessed an eclipse that could take him to a climax. Some of the men would actually come out of the barbershop with chemical process, then known as "conk", still in their hair, melting like butter as it relaxed the natural curl out of their hair. They wouldn't care if their head was burning, as long as they were watching Selena walk until they couldn't see her anymore. They would watch her until she got all the way into her shop. Selena's walk was so cold, so enticing, so hypnotic that one night she went to a club to hear some blues and the rest was history.

Of course, she was a little late, fashionably late, and the show had already started.

She always made an entrance wherever it was.

One day my grandfather, Elmer, Sr., confided in me regarding his divorce from my grandmother. "See that building over there. See those bricks. That's how hard my head was. If I had just listened to her, (my grandmother), it's no telling how far we could've gone together. But I wouldn't listen. I was young and I didn't have anybody to tell me anything positive."

He had some serious regrets. Another time Elmer's regrets were revealed was at my wedding, when he shared his thoughts with my uncle, his former brother-in-law, Paul.

"She sitting up here with her same husband and I'm not with my family." He was referring to his sister, who had played a significant role in him thinking the grass was greener and everything would be sweeter everywhere but where he was. She'd made him feel he could do better than what he actually had with his wife and his children. Although I'm certain he loved his next family, Elmer had multiple regrets. One of his regrets was not being with his first true love, his first wife and their family.

I distinctly remember hearing Elmer trying to prevent one of my brothers from making the same mistake he had made in his younger life. It was a birthday celebration for Elmer and, as usual, my brother was not able to stay. Our grandfather Elmer was not convinced with my brother's flimsy excuse as to why he had to leave early.

"Come here, come here," Elmer Sr. whispered to my brother, who had one foot in the door and the other in the threshold between the apartment and the building's hallway. "Where are you going?" Elmer spoke a little louder. "You've already got the best, right here!"

My brother grinned as he nodded in agreement, shaking Elmer's hand in appreciation of the grandfatherly advice. Elmer pulled his grandson in closer. "You have everything you need right here," he said as he directed his eyes toward my brother's then wife. "I'm telling you. I'm telling you. Listen…It ain't all what you think."

"I hear you, I hear you!" my brother responded as he hugged him and ran out the door anyhow.

Elmer shook his head in disappointment with a wry smile as he stated, "Can't nobody tell him nothing now." He knew, from experience, when the inevitable time came, nobody would be able to soothe his grandson either. The time that day of heartache shows up when the person you took for granted says it's over, realizing they were worth much more than you were able to give.

Another regret my grandfather had was not listening to his first wife, Selena, when she discussed dreams and possibilities for them as a couple, also as a family. He did a lot of yelling, instead of listening. Later, no one held it against him, except maybe himself. Not even Selena. To this day, she will still give him his props for being a good provider, always going to work and bringing her his entire pay check. The problem had been that Selena envisioned more for their future, as a couple, than her husband did. Later in life, Elmer wished he had understood his wife's vision, but, at the time, he was opposed to it. He really didn't see possibility when he was young.

As a result, he missed out on opportunity. Therefore, I grew up feeling sorry for my grandfather. Can you imagine living a life filled with remorse? I feel for anyone living like that. Even if you find someone to fill the empty space, you never find one that can take another's place.

What makes it worse is that when you could have prevented your loss, you had no interest in it. My grandfather didn't want to listen to my grandmother about anything. Especially, when it came to dreams she shared with him about her opening her beauty shop and about him, due to his expertise with cars, opening a gas/service station.

However, he was content with his parking garage job and with my grandmother staying home with the children. His real reason was he didn't want anybody looking at her at all. God forbid, if she went to the grocery store twice in the same day because she had forgotten something. He would growl, "You just going to show yourself!" He was severely jealous.

I guess that was when my grandmother learned one of her lessons in life and, that was, and still is, most times, when a person is constantly accusing you of things like infidelity and other indiscretions, it's usually because of their own behavior and their potential action in the relationship. My grandfather was like Ray Charles and a lot of men who are womanizers.

As the song went, (he) "had a woman way over town," and (he) "couldn't stop loving her," until he realized, like another artist sang, "Your Real Good Thing Is About To End."

In the late 40s, once my grandmother graduated from Madame C.J. Walker's beauty school, she began working in a salon on the Southside in the Pershing Hotel, thus freedom rang. My grandmother, the ravishing enthusiast she was, had been set free. My grandfather's infidelities, his arguing and his drinking had taken its toll on their marriage. I don't think my grandmother, herself, knew just how through she was until men from all directions began offering her help, both financially and emotionally. After she had been divorced, she did have a long-term relationship with one male friend though.

My grandfather should have never let her out of the gate, so to speak. Once Selena finally completed her fifteen hundred hours of beauty culture, she began working for a lady named Ann at a salon on the Southside in the Pershing Hotel.

She went into it as a means to help her husband increase the family income. Though she never considered her or her family to be poor, they had very little.

Whatever they had, though, it was always enough to share. Neighbors would come and borrow a cup of sugar or flour, a couple of eggs, even black pepper until they could get their groceries or promise to pay her back when their husbands got their paycheck, if he was working. Sometimes husbands, more often than not, would pay the debt back. Only a few wouldn't.

Just recently, six decades later, one of the children who lived in the same project, but who had grown into an adult, now living in another state, was in town for a funeral.

However, she did not want to leave for her return home until she reached Selena. The younger woman was thrilled to find Selena alive and well, still boasting a strong mind. She thanked Selena over the phone as she wept with gratitude, explaining and reminiscing how she has never forgotten how nice Selena was to her and her siblings.

She was adamant about not leaving before taking advantage of the opportunity to thank her. The woman continued remembering how hungry she and her siblings would be and how Selena would give them a piece of bread, a roll, a biscuit or make them a sandwich. Depending on what she had left that

day, Selena would always hand them something. There was rarely enough food for leftovers, but if there was anything left and those children or anyone else hungry came to Selena's front or back door, she would divide whatever she had left among them.

There were several children in that particular family. Whenever their father would show up for dinner, which was seldom, he would eat all of whatever it was that their mother had cooked. There was never enough food as it was, but whatever was in the pot, the husband insisted his wife serve him first and he would eat it all—any and everything in the pot that was chewable. He wouldn't leave anything but the juices. He might make a mistake and leave a few scraps of food that you could barely get on a fork in a small amount of pot liquor that was left.

Thank God, my grandfather was nothing like that; he had been a good provider. So much so one of his hell-raising brothers, Bert, called him henpecked because he brought his paycheck home every week and gave it to his wife, my grandmother, to stretch it as far as she could.

Occasionally, Selena would borrow a nickel or two from one of her children's allowance or profit of depositing bottles, but she would always pay them back, her baby daughter, my mother, Juanita, often told me.

Finally, after several years into their fifteen-year marriage, the harassment of Elmer's brother, Bert, invaded my grandfather's spirit. To begin with, Elmer and Selena were both young when they got married, so young that one of their neighbors thought they were sister and brother looking after their younger siblings. In fact, Selena was just a little bit older than the neighbor's oldest daughter. The neighbor would ask "Where is your mother? When is she coming home?"

"My mother doesn't live here," young Selena responded.

"It's just you and your brother?" the neighbor asked inquisitively.

"No, that's my husband."

Then it clicked. A light of recognition shone in the neighbor's eyes. The smaller, younger children were not their little sisters, at least not all of them. Two of the girls were Selena's younger sisters, but the two youngest ones were the couple's children.

My grandfather, Elmer, was the youngest boy of his family. One of his older brothers, Bert, would get drunk and clown. He would curse, fuss and argue his point until the only thing left to do was fight. It always came to blows with him, ending in a knockout, a drag out or a carry out.

All of the Parkers—my grandfather's family—could cuss, as if it were their degreed profession. Consequently, they weren't afraid of a fight. Nevertheless, most of them would walk away from a fight and trouble before Bert would. He was the fighter of the family.

It seemed as though Bert was jealous of his younger brother's relationship with his young wife, Selena.

Bert would often haul off and call Elmer "a henpecked motha-fucka" or "a silly henpecked nigga." Because it was evident that Elmer and his wife were on one accord, loved each other, and were working together in unison to make a nice home for their young family, Bert would nitpick. Selena and Elmer's house, no matter how tiny, was where the family members came to stay when they first arrived in Chicago from Memphis and Mississippi. This included Bert, his wife and their two daughters, who were preteens, just slightly younger than Selena and Elmer.

After being around Bert, Elmer began drinking and cursing, too. I don't know if he was trying to please his big brother, or trying to prove to himself that he was not henpecked. Whatever the case, Elmer's good habits began to deteriorate. Bert was really not a good role model for Elmer.

Bert was so cold, it wasn't long after finding a place for his family to live, he left them. Oddly, Bert's wife was beautiful with glossy long black curly hair slightly tighter than a wave, which some called water wavy hair. Unfortunately, his wife was also very passive. She loved him unconditionally so it hadn't taken much for him to convince her to leave her relatives in Memphis and follow him to Chicago to be near his family.

Though Selena really liked her sister-in-law, she could not understand her excessive passivity and totally submissive behavior. You'll learn later that Selena didn't come from that kind of stock. She's never been the kind of person to roll over and play dead, and ignore her own sense of thought. She always had moxie.

Chapter Two

❧

At the age of three, Selena knew she wanted to do hair. When she was a small child, her mother, Mary, (my maternal great-grandmother,) took her to a neighbor named Miss Bea's house to have her hair done for Easter. Miss Bea did hair in her house and had a reputation for making all of the ladies who patronized her business look pretty.

Over the years, Mary had heard about Miss Bea's salon. She'd seen some of her work on some of her lady friends and decided that she would not only get her hair done, but have her little girl's hair done as well. It was Easter weekend and she didn't feel like the hassle of doing their hair herself.

Although Mary was a sharp dresser and as clean and neat as the white house, she didn't have much patience for styling hair. Ms. Bea pressed Selena's hair and each spiraled curl was as if it were a sculpted ringlet. Back in those days, the Kitchen beautician would use the stove in her own kitchen, which was stacked with wood, to heat the hot comb and the irons. Selena had never seen her hair look so pretty and never felt such spectacular beauty as that day. As young as she was, she knew that she did not want to mess up her hair. She remembered sleeping with her head hanging off the bed and her mother gently lifting her head up and placing it on the pillow with hopes that Selena wouldn't have a crook in her neck in the morning.

The spiral curls, which became known as "Shirley Temple curls," were silky, shiny and bouncy. These were quite different from the corn stalk-looking curls that her mother would create when she attempted to press and curl Selena's hair. My grandmother, Selena, always said that her mother could do anything and make anything better, except her hair. That was because she really didn't care about doing any hair.

Selena never forgot the feeling of pride that she watched the other ladies exhibit and she, herself, felt, as they turned their heads from side to side with inspections of approval while looking in the mirror. Between the meantime, there was the everyday matter of life as she was growing up, a young Black girl in the South.

Chapter Three

During the Depression, around the latter part of 1929 or the early part of 1930, Selena's parents, Mary and Henry Green, moved their family from Friars Point, Mississippi to the outskirts of Lula, before finally settling in Clarksdale, Mississippi, where they both worked in the fields, picking cotton. They were both hardworking hustlers. They not only worked in the fields, but on weekends, they turned their house and a barn, which the owner of the property allowed them to use, into a roadhouse.

Every weekend, Mary would cook chittlin's, greens, cornbread, spaghetti, fried chicken and fish (buffalo was her favorite), Cole slaw and a variety of cobblers, which included peach, blackberry or blueberry. In turn, she'd sell dinners to the folks who would frequent the roadhouse.

After a long week of toiling in the fields, the community would gather at the roadhouse and figuratively "let their hair down." The ladies would be doing dances called "the shimmy" and "the black bottom" to the sounds of Mr. Lit playing the piano like it was invented and designed with him, and only him, in mind. Plenty other musicians would come through often and play their instruments.

In fact, the first time I ever heard Robert Johnson's name was from my grandmother, Selena, when she was reminiscing with my great-grandmother, Granny, (as I called Mary), about the times they had when she and Henry had the road house.

"Them Niggas was there," Granny would say.

Echoing her mother's words, Selena would say to me, "Bonnie, them Negroes was there and Daddy taught Robert Johnson how to pick the guitar."

Yes, they were talking about the famous Robert Johnson Blues singer.

"Daddy could pick the guitar and buck dance, too. He would sound out our names with his feet."

Maybe they shared some skills, but Robert Johnson would be there on the porch, as would many others, picking and singing the blues. As Granny would say, "Them nigga's was playin' the blues, baby, and they could play 'em, too."

From the stories they related, they had big fun back then. Their stories always made my brothers and I wish we had been there. The roadhouse was the happening place to be at in that time and space. There was always plenty of good food, music, dancing, and gambling. They also sold bootleg liquor which Henry would make.

Actually, he would help his boss man make his bootleg liquor to sell and he, in turn, would sell some to Henry at a cheaper price. Sometimes he would leave a little bit for Henry to sifter into a couple of bottles so he could sell a taste, or as some call it, a shot.

The white boss man was decent to Mary and Henry. He liked the way they worked in the fields for him. Mary could pick so much cotton, she picked at least five hundred pounds of cotton a day. She had been picking since she was a young girl living at home with her mama. Even after she had her children, Henry would pull Paul on his sack and Mary would pull Selena, as the youngest, on her sack while they worked the fields picking cotton. The white overseers trusted Mary so much, they hired her to weigh up the cotton that the other pickers would pick.

Mary worked the fields, but she did not work a full day, in order to be able to weigh the cotton for the farm. Some days Mary didn't have to work the fields at all, just weigh the cotton that others picked. Henry worked the fields daily, except for the days that he didn't because he had won big gambling or just didn't feel like it.

As a couple, they made more money because of the road house where they sold bootleg liquor and chittlins. It was then that Selena would look at her mother with pride as she weighed up the cotton after getting out of her own car, a black Model T Ford or the family's midnight blue Packard with the spare on the back. Mary wore custom-made fitted suits and high heels, standing back on her big pretty legs. It was then and there that Selena knew she wanted to be a sharp dresser with custom made clothing just like her mama—when she grew up.

"When I get big, I'm gone dress real pretty like my mama and have my clothes made, too," she would say to herself, her brother, Paul, and anyone else that she saw taking a second look at Mary, as she smiled.

Chapter Four

Unbeknownst to my grandmother, Selena, she experienced her first act of prejudice and segregation, when she was about the age of three.

It was inflicted upon her by her maternal grandmother, Blanche, who had a reputation of being mean and no nonsense to some of her children, the older ones, while being very passive to her younger children. That's why this was different.

Blanche had offered to keep her grandchildren, Paul, then five years old and Selena, then three years old, which made Mary, her daughter, very happy that her mother expressed some interest in her children. Though Blanche's youngest child was just a year older than Paul, she had never babysat her grandchildren. Of course, they knew their "Big Mama" and would visit her with their mother, Mary. Then they would see Blanche, along with her husband, Mary's stepfather, Mr. Will, and their aunts and uncles, but they would always leave with their mother when she left.

Over the years, Mary noticed that Blanche had become more lenient with her younger siblings (the second set of children), and she was so elated with the idea of Blanche wanting to keep her children, she said okay. She kissed her little ones goodbye that evening and went on home to tell Henry the news about her mama offering to keep the children. He wasn't as thrilled about it as Mary, but he was shocked.

The next day, Mary and Henry picked up their children, who were running and playing happily around the house until they heard their parents' voices.

They were so ecstatic, they each jumped into their parents' arms.

Henry asked, "Did you have a good time?"

Little Selena was bursting with excitement to tell her Daddy what a good time they had with Big Mama.

"We had fun, Daddy. Paul slept in the bed with Big Mama and I slept on the floor. It was fun."

Henry's brow furrowed. He didn't like what he thought he heard. He turned and asked Selena, "You slept where?"

Selena excitedly repeated that Big Mama had her to sleep on the floor.

Instantly, Henry became furious. He immediately stood up while holding Selena in his arms. Speaking with sincere authority, he vowed that his children would never stay overnight or be left in Blanche's care ever again. In no uncertain terms, he told his mother-in-law how low down he thought she was for making his baby girl sleep on the floor.

Meantime, Selena had no idea why her daddy was so upset, but, as she continued to listen to him, all the while noticing the hurt in both her parents' eyes, she understood that there was something wrong.

Henry was a tall, dark, handsome man so he was well aware of the reason that Blanche allowed "Sunman" (Paul), who was two years older than his sister, sleep in the bed with her. Sunman was lighter than Selena, who was dark like Henry. In fact, Mary would often call her "my pretty chocolate doll."

Even the sadness in Mary's eyes expressing the question, "Why?" with tear-stained eyes didn't provoke any visual remorse from Blanche. Blanche, who was mixed with Indian, was fair-skinned, and had long hair. She was short and petite. She acted as though she didn't know what they were insinuating. I was always kind of confused about that accusation because Blanche's first husband, Wash, had been brown skinned.

My grandmother, Selena, cleared it up as she remembered it did, in fact, happen. She went on to state that she was indeed darker than her brother, Paul, but that never mattered to the two of them because it never made a difference in their household. Whether it's racial, interracial or biracial, people are taught all of the "self-limiting" isms," (such as racism or intra-racism), when you are exposed to that type of learned behavior, you act accordingly, unless you are taught otherwise. Mary and Henry loved all of their children. They had two children at the time, and eight years later, had two more daughters. They didn't make any difference in them, nor did they allow anyone else to breed that poison in them by making a difference, not even their grandmother.

Ironically, it wasn't too long after that Paul's skin turned darker from a severe bout with scarlet fever. Soon he was up running and playing with his sister again, and there was no difference to be made. Selena and her big brother, Paul, always loved one another.

Chapter Five

For at least eight years, it was just the two children, Paul and Selena, and they were as thick as buttermilk. Their parents still picking cotton and hustling on the weekends making their money at the roadhouse afforded them the luxury of an automobile. One time, while they were riding in their Model T Ford with Daddy, when Paul was about five years old, Selena almost four, the car flipped over onto its side. As the car turned over, it threw Paul across the field on the dirt road and had Selena and her father pinned underneath it. The fender of the car was resting on little Selena's neck.

My grandmother, Selena, still laughs as she tells the story today. While admitting it wasn't funny at the time, it was frightening as she screamed out for her daddy to rescue her and he did.

The tall, healthy, strong man that her Daddy, Henry was, he quickly and gently positioned himself, using the weight of his body through his shoulders and arms, then lifted the car off of his baby girl's neck, just enough for him to use one arm to assist her in squirming her way from underneath it.

My grandmother remembered the funny part was Paul sitting across the road where he had been thrown, rubbing his head as he watched his dad trying to get the car's fender off of his sister. The first thing that came to Paul's mind came out of his mouth; he looked at the car as he said, "That motherfucker!"

Her daddy was so relieved to get the fender off of Selena's neck and that both he and his children were okay, he didn't even chastise Paul. Silently and secretly, he probably agreed with him.

❦

As children, Selena and Paul were together all of the time. What happened to one, if it didn't happen to the other one, they witnessed it. There was the time when the traveling circus was in town and they saw how good Selena and Paul could dance, they took them with them to be a part of the act. Fortunately, a neighbor saw them leading the two children away with them and ran to get Mary and Henry.

"Mary, Henry, come quick!" Miss Angie, the neighbor, shouted with as much breath as she could after running all the way to their house. Miss Angie was the neighbor lady who made cakes all through the year. At holiday time, especially Christmas, she would make even more cakes, all kinds, lemon cakes, caramel, butter pound cake, chocolate, and coconut. She made enough cakes to last from December to July, which is when Selena would run to her house and announce that it was her birthday and ask for a piece.

Miss Angie, one of two ladies who really made a lasting impression on Selena as a child, would always have a slice of cake for all of the children, especially Selena. Ms. Angie had just pulled one of her lemon cakes from the trunk she stored the well wrapped cakes in on her porch when she happened to look up and saw the tent being taken down and the wagons being loaded with all of the circus's belongings. However, when she saw the white folks reaching for Selena and Paul, Ms. Angie dropped that cake on top of that trunk and ran to Mary and Henry's house just down the way from hers.

Mary and Henry ran and caught up with them; they hadn't gotten far. After the ringmaster and the manager finished pleading, explaining what great dancers their children were and how much money they could send home, Mary still told them no—she might have told them hell no. She was feisty and ready to kill or be killed for her children. Walking away with both children in tow, she fussed at Selena and Paul a bit, as she told them she sent them to see the circus, not to join it. The only reason she let them go in the first place is because you could see the circus tent from their house but, thank goodness, it was closer to Ms. Angie's.

Selena and Paul both were thrilled that the circus people enjoyed their dancing, but, nonetheless, they were strangers. Afterwards, Mary and Henry made sure they understood that clearly. Mary was so relieved that she and Henry had caught up with the people from the circus when she got her children safely back inside of their little shot gun house, you could see the sigh of relief flow through her entire body. It would be years before she would let Selena and Paul out of her sight again.

Years later, after Selena and Paul had grown a little older, their mama, Mary, allowed them to walk to Lula, Mississippi, which was the closest town to where they lived at the time, to pick and buy their own Easter shoes. The two of them were so excited; they felt like they were finally growing up, almost grown even, by their mama allowing them to go shopping alone. Selena chose some black satin back pumps. Not only were they too grown for a young girl still young enough to be on program to recite an Easter speech, but they hurt like hell, she could barely walk in the future stilettos and they made her feel as though she looked like a clown, towering over the other children. Being a tall young girl naturally in her bare feet, she didn't need, or want, to be any taller. Selena realized this before she ever made it to church, but it was too late. She picked them, she paid for them and brought them all the way back home.

Mary made her wear the shoes with her white ankle sox. Selena's feet hurt so badly she forgot her Easter speech. The combination of embarrassment and aching feet convinced Selena not to buy or wear high heels until she was really grown—at least thirty-five—and even then she didn't wear too high of a heel, perhaps just two to two-and-three-quarters inch heels. Meantime, the toes on Paul's shoes were so pointed and hurt him so bad, he threw them away after suffering with blistered feet that Easter Sunday evening.

The following Sunday Paul had on his old worn shoes again. When Mary asked him where his new shoes were, he made up a lie, telling her that he left them out in the field one day when he was helping his daddy. When it was time to leave the field, he could not find them anywhere. Mary fussed as she told him and Selena that they did not have any money to waste on shoes they couldn't wear just because they liked how they looked. Next time, they had better know that they would be able to wear them and not for a couple of minutes, either, but for a while, for instance all day for the remainder of the year.

Chapter Six

Selena insists to this day that she would not change a thing in her life. She often says that If she had to do it all over, she would travel the same road again because the experiences that her life lessons taught her were a blessing and made her that much stronger as a woman and as a human being. Selena was, and is, a born survivor.

A great deal of Selena's survival instincts were instilled in her by her parents, especially her mother, Mary, who guided and reared her children with prayer and faith, while leaning and depending on the presence of God. God instills in each one of us all that we need to survive in life. It's up to each one of us to tap into it by being open and receptive to His guidance.

As human nature would have it, Selena would and did make some mistakes but she learned from them. In other words, her mistakes in life didn't stop her from persevering. She didn't give up; Selena is not, and never has been, a quitter.

To this day, she remembers situations and conversations she witnessed as a child that she learned from and would carry with her all through life.

From the time she was young girl herself, Selena has always been extremely caring and sensitive to senior citizens and children. To this day, she hates to see or hear about anyone being mistreated, but she believes older people and children are more helpless, more vulnerable to the misgivings of otherwise grown, mischievous souls, disguised as human beings. I say disguised because God gives us all five senses and one of those senses is the sense of empathy. Just as some people are born without a physical limb, some people are born devoid of feelings for others.

It's hard to believe that there are some who sit and ponder ways to hurt others. Sometimes, it's due to some circumstance that caused the victimizer to be hurt or disappointed and they simply want to retaliate, but sometimes, let's face it. There are just some evil, angry, unhappy folk, mad (in the crazy sense) enough to want to hurt and harm others, just to see them suffer. That's when you know there is some type of deficiency; something is missing. Most times what is missing is their sense of feelings, and if that is missing, they have no ability to care. Enough of that; the doctor has left the building.

Selena's heart strings are really pulled when she hears of a child who has been abandoned by its mother, for whatever reason. Although her mother never abandoned her, she does recall one of the times her parents separated. Her mother left and went to Memphis to stay with family for a couple of weeks, leaving Selena and Paul with Henry. Selena remembers her mother had cooked them a good breakfast, bacon, eggs, grits and biscuits. Selena ate all of her food, as did Paul and Henry. Mary got ready to go. As she kissed her children goodbye, she told them she would see them soon. Later that evening, Selena noticed it was past time for her mother to be home. She began to ask her dad, Henry, when was her mama coming home and where was she. He would only answer, "She be home soon."

Back then, adults didn't do a lot of explaining, and, likewise, children knew not to ask too many questions.

Henry wasn't too good of a cook, but he managed to fry them some salt pork and corn for dinner. For breakfast, he boiled some grits to eat with some leftover salt pork. Selena still had one of the biscuits she had kept from the last meal her mother had cooked for them before she left a couple of days ago. As much as she missed her mother, she believed her mother was coming back. She wanted to be able to show her mother that she was a big girl and could take care of herself by doing things the way she saw her mother do them so she tried.

Selena would often get the nettle rash and her mother would give her a broken dose of Epson salt. During the two weeks Mary was gone Selena began to itch on her neck and arm. She had what they called "the nettle rash" again. She thought to herself, *I know what to do. I'm gone take a broken dose of Epson salt like Mama gave me.* Selena had no idea what a broken dose was so her interpretation was far too much.

Selena's broken dose turned into an overdose. She poured and poured, Epson salt and water, water and Epson salt. She took her time and stirred it just before drinking every drop of it. By this time, Henry was in the fields working. Paul was somewhere playing outdoors; Selena went to join him, but as she ran farther out into the field, her vision started to blur. In a matter of minutes, her sight went from blurry to complete blindness. Selena was crawling around in the field, blind, feeling her way for God knows how long, before a man, who was an acquaintance of Henry's, happened to see her. It didn't take him long to realize that she did not recognize him by the way she was feeling around for the ground. She was almost to the river when he picked her up and carried her to her daddy, Henry, who was still working in the field.

Circumstances such as this one are probably what prompted the "keep out of reach of children" disclaimer that adorns just about everything, medications, cleaning products and various other poisonous and hazardous products. Henry took Selena from the gentleman's arms and began asking her what happened, what was wrong, as he tried not to panic. Noticing the urgency in her father's voice and missing the sound of her mother's voice stirred the fear in little Selena as she began trembling. She spoke in a chanting rhythm, "I can't see, I can't see, Daddy."

A little while after being reunited with her daddy and a few trips to the outhouse, Selena regained her sight. Henry carried Selena back to the house and laid her down on her bed for a while. Just before closing her eyes, she made sure that the biscuit she had been saving was still under her pillow, she promised herself she would keep it until her mama came home. Later, the next day Selena was up, playing around as usual.

A few days later, Granny Mary returned home from Memphis. Back in those days, people hardly had enough money to get to and from where they had been. It was a blessing for them and their love ones just to have them return. There are always exceptions to the rule, and Selena's mother, Mary, was one of them. She was always a thoughtful person and God blessed her for her generosity.

For decades and years to come, whatever anyone needed at anytime, anywhere she had it in her pocketbook. Her purse was never junky or heavy but it was filled with tender. If you needed a piece of change, or love, if you needed a handkerchief for tearstained eyes or a runny nose, Mary was always there. She took time to care if your slip was hanging or the hem came out of your dress, skirt or pants or perhaps your button popped, she definitely had a safety pin or two.

This time she thought about her babies, waiting at home for her, and she brought them back some candy from the complementary candy dish at the hotel where her sister, Lucy, worked in the kitchen in Memphis as one of the head cooks.

Mary had calmed down after almost two weeks. She was even glad to see her husband, Henry, whom she had been angry with for staying out all night gambling. Most times, he won but not this time. In fact, he almost lost twice, both his money and his wife. Within the week, things began to normalize. They fell back into their same routine. Selena's parents were picking cotton in the fields while Selena and her brother, Paul, were anticipating starting their second and third year of school, which was held at their church. The church house was also the schoolhouse. They were both excited about learning. Back then they called it, "Getting your lesson."

"You better get your lesson," one elder might say, or if you had homework, "Have you finished getting your lesson?"

Selena and Paul both could do their numbers, they could do their figures. Selena loved her spelling more than anything. She could spell better than most of the children. She would be one of the first ones up for the spelling contest and one of the last ones to sit down. Most times she was the winner.

In between the routine of Mama and Daddy working, and Selena and Paul getting their lessons, there was playtime. Sometimes Selena and Paul would play together, while other times, Paul would be off playing with some other little boys. Meantime, Selena would be playing with the little Mullenlaw girls, the daughters of the boss man, owner of the plantation where Mary and Henry lived and picked cotton. The three girls played together often, but one day the two Mullenlaw sisters changed the game when they decided to spit on little Selena.

Selena was too young to think about any kind of "rules," "Jim Crow," or any other "white is right, black get back" idiosyncrasies pertaining to Negroes and Whites. Selena acted on the impulse of being violated and grabbed both girls by the back of their heads. With her hands entangled in their long blonde hair, she butted their heads together continuously until their mother came out and pried Selena's hands out of her daughters' hair.

"Selena!" Mrs. Mullenlaw screamed. "What are you doing? Stop, no, no, no. Why are you doing this?"

"They spit on me, they spit on me," Selena shouted as she ran home to tell her mother.

It would be a while before they played together again. They must have missed playing with Selena because one day the three of them, the mother and the two girls, came to Henry and Mary's house to apologize. They begged Selena's pardon as they promised both the little girl and her mother, Mary, that nothing like that would ever happen again.

"Please come and play with us, Selena," the girls pleaded. She did, but not before she gave them a look of silent instruction, which made them know that they better not try anything. Selena didn't like fighting. She wasn't accustomed to it, but she wasn't going to let those girls bully her.

I guess bullies have existed since the beginning of time. I know I have escaped from a few. Either you were a bully, a runner, or an instigator, unless you had a mother like my grandmother had. You had to fight back in order for her not to jump you and that was a fight that you were sure to lose. I thank God my mother was not like that.

It became a matter of survival for Selena when a girl named Fannie Ray became her school nightmare.

Everyday Fannie Ray would push Selena, bump her, or kick dirt on Selena's clean white sox. Instead of retaliating, Selena would respond, "I don't want to fight, Fannie Ray."

Selena had a friend and playmate named Dolly. Both she and Paul, were so fed up with the way Selena was allowing this bully, Fannie Ray, to get away with this constant tormenting that they told Selena's mother, Mary Green.

Dolly started talking about the bully incidents with Paul in the yard. They were near the clothing line where Ms. Green hung up clothes. Their mother would be able to hear the conversation, without Paul or Dolly straight out telling on Selena.

"Paul, why won't Selena speak up for herself when Fannie Ray kicking that dirt on her sox?"

Paul was glad Dolly brought the subject up in hearing distance of his mother's ears. Although he did not want to tell on his sister, he wanted her to stop letting that girl get away with picking on her because he knew Selena could whip her. I guess Selena herself had doubts though. Selena just stood there, looking sheepish as they discussed her predicament.

Paul responded to Dollie, "I don't know why Selena keep letting Fannie Ray bump her and push her around. I know she can whip her."

Selena's mama hung the last bit of clothes on the line to dry, then asked Dolly and Paul what they were talking about. After fake anticipation, the two children repeated themselves in unison.

"This girl named Fannie Ray be picking on Selena and gettin' in her face and Selena don't do nothin' 'bout it."

Mama became so livid, she called Selena over closer to her. "If you don't beat Fannie Ray's ass the next time she touches you, I'm going to beat yours!"

Mary made it clear to Paul that he better let her know. Selena knew her mama meant that.

Chapter Seven

A couple of days later, the kids were talking about how Fannie Ray really wanted to fight Selena. Selena was out on the school grounds with her jelly bucket. Let me explain. A jelly bucket was a small bucket made from tin with a handle around it. Ordinarily, jelly would come packed in it, but when they were emptied and the jelly was all gone, Mama would clean and use them to put Selena and Paul's lunches in for school.

That day, Fannie Ray walked up to Selena with a crowd of instigators and onlookers. Selena turned to face Fannie. The kids she was interacting with began to make a circle around the two girls. One of the children from the crowd stepped forward and placed a straw on Selena and Fannie Ray's shoulder. Stepping back out of the way like a referee, the straw girl stated, "Now y'all know whoever knocks the straw off the other one first starts the fight!"

The circle of instigators chanted, "Go on Selena!" or "Go on Fannie Ray!" and "Fight, fight!"

Before she knew it, Fannie Ray knocked Selena's straw off first, but this time Selena went ballistic. She was like a human tornado striking everything that came under the jelly bucket from Fannie Ray to the teacher who tried to stop the fight. Selena's fear had transformed her into a crazy girl; she beat Fannie's you-know-what like her mama told her to and the teacher's behind, too. Anything that came under the jelly bucket, she whipped.

The next day, the teacher made them walk in front of the class back and forth until they made friends. The day after that,

Fannie brought Selena some flowers she had picked as a peace offering. Or, she offered them as a plea of insurance not to ever have another ass whipping by her new friend, Selena, again; take your pick.

Afterwards, Paul and Dolly were pleased to tell Mama how Selena had whipped Fannie Ray.

Selena still laughs when she tells the story about Uncle Paul and his bully.

This boy was bigger and older than Paul and he picked a fight with Paul every day. Even so, Paul would fight him back. The bully was so much stronger than Paul, Paul was never satisfied with standing up to him. He wanted to get the best of the boy.

Paul wanted to win the fight. To some, Paul had won some of the fights. But Paul felt if he had, the boy wouldn't keep coming back for more. Paul wanted to stop him for good. In all honesty, Paul was probably tired of being beaten. The last time the bully thought to antagonize Paul, he was horrified when Paul came to school swinging a two-bitted ax. Paul, around ten or eleven, no more than twelve years of age, swung that ax back and forth like a scale needle waves when one first gets on it. The teachers pleaded with Paul to give them the ax, but he would not release it. They begged and pleaded with him to simply put it down, he would not. They called him by his first name, then his full name.

"Paul, give me the ax," one teacher asked in a calm tone

"Paul, come now. We know you don't want to hurt anyone. Give us the ax and we can talk about it," the other teacher spoke from a distance.

Paul continued to swing the ax back and forth, round and round.

"Paul Green, please put the ax down before you hurt yourself or someone else!" the teachers shouted as they assisted the frightened, scattered children inside.

To no avail, they approached his sister, Selena.

"Selena, can't you get him to give the ax to you, or at least convince him to put it down?"

"No, Ma'am, he'll hit a baby." Selena spoke from a distance.

Once the teachers found out why Paul had the ax in the first place, they were able to assure him that the bully, "Theodis," would not bother him anymore. Still, Paul did not relinquish the ax, but he did stop swinging it and no one got close to him the rest of the day.

Of course, his mother had to take Paul to school the next day, as well as Theodis's mother, to meet with the teachers and resolve this issue. If the boys wanted to continue school and not be forced to work the fields all year, they had to agree not to fight anymore.

❧

A year or so later, Selena and Paul had a brand new baby sister, Earline. A year or two after that, their second baby sister, Eileen, was born. Selena loved all of her siblings. She was not only Paul's best buddy, she was a nurturing, protective big sister to her two younger sisters. Of the older two siblings, Selena and Paul, Selena always exhibited more sensitivity. Selena had a sense of mother wit at the tender young age of eight-and-a-half when the first of the two little sisters was born. Now ten years of age, when her youngest baby sister was born, Selena was the big sister to the two of them.

As life would have it, she was Paul's big sister, too, at times, even though he was the firstborn to Henry and Mary. Selena would help her mother in any way she could with her two younger siblings. The elder baby sister was really afraid of water and Mary would run out of patience. Selena would intervene, "Mama, let me do it. Don't whip her. I'll bathe her."

Mary would sit to the side and let Selena persuade her little sister not to be afraid of the water as she made a game out of demonstrating a little fun by gently splashing in the water.

Chapter Eight

A few years later, Selena's mama and daddy separated for the last and final time. As the years had gone by, Henry only wanted to gamble. He was tired of working in the field so he stopped going in at all. From that point on, Selena became her mom's little helper more so than ever. After leaving Henry, Mary moved her children to Memphis, Tennessee.

Subsequently, she found a job doing day work as a domestic, making fifty cents a week. Mary's first cousin, Booker, and his wife took Mary and her four children in until she was able to get her own place. It took her a year, but she did.

Right after the family moved in, Cousin Booker walked Mary and her children down to the grocery store, which they lived up over and explained to the store merchant (who was also the landlord) that they were his relatives. He let him know that he and Mary were two sisters' children. From that point on, the landlord never complained about them being there or charged extra rent.

"If they need anything at all," he said, "please let them have it. I will take care of it." He gave his word and kept his word, what a man.

Selena always loved and remembered her cousin Booker for not only being so nice to them as children, but for being nice to their mama and easing her mind as she worked to provide a living for her four young children. One lesson Mary taught her children by her example was to never give up; she was a proud and independent woman. She never asked for welfare to care for her children. She worked on her hands and knees, scrubbing white folks' houses, and never complained.

Sometimes, when the food supply was short, they might have to eat oatmeal three times a day, but they never went hungry. Even if the children were at a neighbor's house, they knew better than to act, or look, as though they were hungry.

"Mama said if you could make a turd or go to the bathroom, you had eaten and you were full," Selena recalled.

Young Selena, who was thirteen or fourteen, would see women outside washing and hanging clothes on a line while her mother was at work. Imitating them, she would get a chair and stand in it to hang her family's clothes on the line. She worked hard, trying to ease her mother's load of responsibility, so much so that a knot, some referred to as a win, grew on her arm.

Once she surprised her mama by baking a cake, but that didn't go too well. Selena used so much baking powder and flour that it rose so big that it expanded to the size of the entire oven and was still growing when her mother opened the oven. It scared her immensely. For a fleeting second, she wanted to whip Selena, but she knew deep inside that her little girl did it from her heart. She was only trying to make her mother happy by showing that she was her big girl she could count on. Mary thanked Selena, but she made her little girl promise never to cook again unless Mama was home. Selena promised as she looked with amazement through her big bright eyes.

Selena and Paul's school was on Lauderdale and Iowa Street. Before school, the two would walk their two younger sisters to school where Ms. Potts was their kindergarten teacher on Mississippi Boulevard. That happened to be the same street where a young lady named Gladys of Gladys' Luncheonette in Chicago started her well known, mojo working, never disappointing restaurants by selling dinners off of a bus right there in Memphis. To this day, Selena remembers passing that bus with the aroma of good smelling, home-cooked food dancing around her nose as she walked down Mississippi Boulevard, taking her sisters to and from school. Selena and Gladys' paths would cross again in later years.

As the children of divorce, Selena was a brand new teenager, when she began to travel back and forth with her brother, Paul, to visit their daddy, Henry, in Mississippi. Henry had returned to the fields for work. Paul would work in the field with Daddy while they were visiting. Meanwhile, Selena would stay around the house because she was terrified of snakes and they were prevalent in the fields.

Selena would take water and lunch close to the field for Daddy and Paul, yet she didn't go too close. She would holler way off in the distance. "Daddy, Daddy, supper!"

She would hold the food up in the air and scan the grounds surrounding her, watching for snakes. One day Selena arrived back from taking Daddy and Paul his lunch just in time to see a boy named JW. He was a handsome young man, who had a pretty car, but on this particular day, his car had stopped and he had to walk to get some help. Through happenstance, the road he took ribboned right past Selena's daddy's house.

Selena was outside washing clothes in a wash tub on a wash board when she noticed a familiar face walking toward her. He smiled as he approached the pretty, shapely-built girl, maybe they were acquaintances or maybe they were friends. Perhaps they even had a secret crush on each other. One thing for sure; they were two young people, one boy and one girl, and each thought the other one was good looking. With no adult supervision in sight, obviously their curiosity was piqued; their hormones were raging. JW was running his sweet plea, talking game filled with compliments, to young Selena. He told her how he had always liked her. Selena was about fourteen years of age by then, and JW was a few years older than her. They were alone in her father's house.

Young girls are usually quite smitten by older boys anyway. Selena was enamored by his good looks and gentle persuasion. She had no idea of the consequences she would incur from the brief moments of affectionate lust she experienced for the first time. Selena had no idea, I mean not a clue, that she could become pregnant because her mother didn't talk about anything pertaining to sex.

Back in those days, parents rarely, if ever, talked about anything concerning making babies or fleshly pleasures. That was considered "grown folks business." Selena and JW would see each other a few more times before Selena and her brother Paul returned to Memphis where their mother and two younger sisters were. They would grin and talk and sneak a chance to hold hands, but they were never alone again.

Chapter Nine

Being a single mother, working day and night, trying to feed her four children, it took some time before Mary noticed. Six months passed; Selena began to gain weight and her mother finally figured it out. She didn't know when, where, how or who, but she knew her daughter's belly was growing. The baby was just about due by this time. Selena remembered taking her usual bath in the tin wash tub that the family had and noticing her stomach getting bigger, but she didn't know why.

Mary never, ever talked to Selena about anything. Selena didn't know about sex and its relationship to making babies. She didn't even know about her monthly period, until it happened. I guess some parents, especially back in those days, felt if they did not speak about those things, there was a better chance that nothing would happen. They acted as if their children, especially their girls, didn't know anything, they couldn't or wouldn't do anything…so much for that theory.

"WHO DID YOU GO WITH"? Mary yelled at Selena while looking at her stomach. Selena didn't even know what that meant.

Mama's voice went up a few more octaves. "Did you lay down with somebody? Who did you lay down with? Who was it?"

Selena began to tell her about JW coming by Daddy's house because his car had stopped and Daddy and Paul were out in the field working. Mama didn't say much more to her, except that she would have to write and tell the boy. She instructed her to wait until the baby was born, which wouldn't be long and send a picture.

Mary had the wind knocked out of her, knowing the difficulties she faced as a single mother, trying to feed her four children and herself while making fifty cents a week doing domestic work, but she cow girled up and did what she knew how to do. She worked hard, prayed and trusted in God.

Once he realized that Mary was not coming back to him or Mississippi. Henry sent money to Mary in Memphis from his wages he received from working in the fields. Cousin Booker was still one of God's angel's helping Mary feed her children and helping in any other way that he could.

Mary wrote and told Henry about their daughter's pregnancy. He was shocked, but he increased his financial support as often as he could.

Paul was old enough to help out now and he got a job working at the drug store, making deliveries, where he met and made a new friend, Elmer Parker. Elmer had a bike that he used to make his deliveries and get around. As Elmer and Paul's friendship grew stronger, they became real buddies.

The drugstore was owned by a white husband and wife who had a baby. By this time Selena had stopped going to school in the ninth grade. She would stay home most of the time, but she would go to work with her brother, Paul, to get out of the house. The store owner began paying Selena to watch her baby, which allowed the store owner a little more freedom to help her husband in the store. Selena would play with the baby, rock or push the baby around in the buggy for a while.

That is when Paul introduced his sister, Selena, to his new friend, Elmer. Overnight, it seemed, the three of them became tight. Paul and Selena took him home to meet Mama and their two younger sisters. Sometimes he would eat supper with them; sometimes he wouldn't out of fear that he would wear out his welcome. Though Mary didn't have much, she would always offer to share whatever she had with him and anybody else.

Elmer liked his new friends. He liked that they were a family. Most of all, he loved the way they treated him. He began to feel a part of their family, but who he liked the most was Selena. She was pretty to him and his heart went out to her as a young girl pregnant, whereas whoever the man or the boy responsible was virtually invisible. There was no one in sight ever, not even a mention of whom the father could be, until Elmer asked. Selena explained that the boy lived in Mississippi. According to her, the putative father was a nice person, who didn't know that she was pregnant. However, Selena assured Elmer once the father found out about the impending birth, he would help her take care of their baby.

To Elmer, the coast wasn't totally clear, but he couldn't stop his heartfelt feelings from growing for Selena and her unborn child. He was very attentive to her whenever he was around her, which was every day as Elmer, Paul and Selena would walk home together. On the days that Selena didn't work, Elmer would still walk with Paul, rolling his bike alongside of him, just to be able to see Selena.

Selena thought of Elmer as a real nice person and a good friend. In fact, she liked him. She liked the way he treated her, but she had reservations when it came to Elmer. For one, she thought as soon as JW and his family found out about the baby, they would probably get married. At the very least, they would see to it that she and the baby were taken care of. JW's family was a "light-skinned," good-looking people. They were really well off, with plenty of everything, which included their own land, their own farm animals, their own equipment, and their own money in the bank. Moreover, they were well respected in the community.

As the time drew nearer for the baby to arrive, Selena stayed close to home. Mary still had not prepared Selena for what to expect during child birth. Miss Mabel, a next door neighbor, knew that Mary had not really spoken to fifteen-year-old Selena about what to expect because of the unspoken rituals of "don't talk, don't tell" that were so familiar back then. Perhaps it was out of shame and embarrassment that Mary didn't want to speak about it because it was extremely hard in those days for a woman, not to mention a young girl, fourteen or fifteen years old, to be pregnant, about to give birth out of wedlock. Selena, herself, was practically a baby.

One day Ms. Mabel saw Selena outside and took it upon herself to tell young Selena that her water was going to break when the time came for the baby. Again Selena was clueless as to what she meant. "What?" she asked, dumbfounded.

Miss Mabel continued to try and explain it to her, telling her that a gush of water would come out of her when the baby was ready to come. Selena then wondered exactly where the baby was going to come from.

Ms. Mabel told her, "It's going to come out the same way it got in there. It's going to come out of your bottom."

Ms. Mabel could see the uncertainty in Selena's face so she reiterated...

"It's going to come out of your behind, child."

Perplexed, Selena didn't know what that meant.

The time had finally come and Selena went into in labor. Mr. Fred, a friend of Mary's, drove Mary and Selena to the hospital in his automobile. The nurses took Selena into a room and prepared her for the doctor. After the doctor examined Selena, he told everyone, "Yes, it really is time. The baby is on its way, but she needs to dilate a few more centimeters." With that, he left the room. Two nurses monitored Selena until it was time.

Selena thought the time was closer because it felt like her water was about to break. A gush of fluid did come out of her, but it was not her water breaking. Actually, she had to go to the bathroom. She peed all over the nurses. They screamed in shock as Selena chanted, "My water broke, my water broke, my water broke."

Realizing the young girl did not know any better, the two nurses informed her that her water did not break. Instead, she had indeed urinated on them. The look of shock and shame on Selena's face helped them to see the humor of the situation. The nurses laughed and young Selena was relieved that they were not angry with her. A little while later, her water did break and she gave birth to a beautiful baby girl, Delores, whom she nicknamed Dee- Dee. That was the beginning of a real love affair, family style. Selena loved and adored her firstborn, Mary loved her first grandbaby and Elmer couldn't have loved her anymore if she had been his own flesh and blood. No one outside of the family knew anything else, but she was his, Elmer's baby girl, he made sure of that.

Later, my grandmother would warn me against premarital sex by saying, "Having a baby will burst your behind open wider than an oat sack." So it is easy to assume her birth with her first child as a young teen mother was difficult.

Anyhow, Selena remained in the hospital a few more days before returning home. Upon her return home, Selena took a while to recover. Considering her young age, the experience of childbirth proved to be a traumatic one and she was still feeling bad. In fact, she fainted. When she came to, she was lying on her bed surrounded by her two best friends, her mama, Mary, and Elmer, trying to give her some water. It meant a lot to her that Elmer was there for her and her new baby girl.

This was a new season in her life and she was experiencing a lot of different emotions, one of which was fear. Not knowing what the future would be like for her and this small person whom she was now responsible for, was a lot for her to think about. One thing that eased her mind was the love, support and guidance of her mother. However, she did see Elmer in a different light. She appreciated him being there on that day when she was feeling so sick. His kindness really touched her heart.

Chapter Ten

The baby was almost six weeks old and Selena was feeling much better. Every afternoon when he finished his deliveries, Elmer had been there to help Mary take care of Selena and the new addition to the family.

Selena had not forgotten what her mother told her about writing and sending a picture of the baby to JW. At the time of her and the baby's six week check-up, Mary took Selena to the doctor. Both Selena and the baby received a good report from the doctor. Afterwards, they stopped at the drugstore to have a picture of the baby made.

Mary had already picked up a stamp and an envelope for Selena the day before. When they returned home, Mary changed clothes, washed her hands and began making preparations for supper while Selena put the baby in her bassinet. She sat at the kitchen table to start writing the note to JW. The baby girl looked just like him. Selena was filled with enthusiasm and excitement, just knowing that JW and his family would be thrilled with how much the baby looked like him. Selena showed the note to her mother and her mother gave her an approving nod as she stirred the batter for her hot water cornbread that she was preparing to go with the nickel's worth of neck bones she had cooked.

Just before sealing the envelope, Selena signed the note, signed the picture complete with the baby's date of birth and how much she weighed on the back of it. Three generations of hope were sealed in that envelope: Mary was hoping for her young daughter and new granddaughter's sake that the father and his family would be respectful and decent enough to accept some of the responsibility. After all, he was older than Selena by a few years. Selena was hoping that as much as he professed that he had always liked her, he might want to marry her and take care of her and his baby girl that looked so much like him. She hoped if nothing else, he would want to make sure that his baby was provided for, seeing that he and his family wanted for nothing and she was a part of them.

As for the baby, she was the innocent pawn in this scenario. Babies grow up to be children who have unconditional trust that they are loved. Intuitively, they hope to belong to someone, usually a mother and a father, once they find out that's how it should be.

The next morning, Selena, full of hope, gave the letter to the postman. About two weeks later, Selena received a letter in the mail. Filled with enthusiasm and anticipation, Selena opened the envelope, looking for a positive response. Instead what she found was the picture that she had sent two weeks before. There was nothing else in the envelope; no acknowledgement at all.

Talk about growing pains. The birth of her child was a growing pain, but when Selena opened that envelope that was addressed by JW's mother and saw the picture of her baby girl returned to her, something rose up in her. Something inside of her turned and churned. She grew up and was changed in a matter of moments.

After realizing and digesting what it meant to have the picture returned without an utter of concern, she was changed for life. Selena vowed that they would never hear from her and her baby again and she kept that promise to herself. She never tried to contact JW or his family again, not ever. As long as she had her mother and her mother's guidance teaching her to lean and depend on God, she knew everything would be all right for her and her baby.

As disappointed and let down as Selena felt at that time, she was not devastated by this blow. She could have been disillusioned for life. But she wasn't. First of all, she was raised in the church and had witnessed her mother's undying faith. But now it was time for her to exercise her own faith muscles. A new spirit was born in her that day—the spirit of determination. Selena was determined that with God's help, she would make it anyhow because of God's will. She truly believed God can make a way when and where there seems to be no way.

Meantime, Elmer's loyalty had not wavered. He continued to come by every day to visit with Selena and help out in any way that he could. He even taught her younger sisters how to tell time. He became a second big brother to them. Even when Elmer and Paul would play ball together, they'd look out for one another just like brothers. A couple of months had passed and Elmer finally made the decision to ask Selena to marry him. The attention he had given her and her baby girl was so kind, it was as if it were his baby. Not only was he in their home on a daily basis, anything that Selena, the baby, or Mama needed, he would do his best to get it or help get it. He was a young guy himself. He was just a few years older than Selena, but he was a hard working young man. Selena had studied all of his good qualities and she was sure of one thing; she really liked the way he treated her. He was in her corner. When he asked her would she marry him, Selena answered, "Yes," to his proposal. Next, together they asked Mama for her permission on their marriage as Selena was still under age.

All along, Mama had noticed how nice and attentive Elmer was to both her daughter and her granddaughter. She felt like he was one of the family. She had grown to really favor and appreciate him like a second son. Thus, Mama gave them her blessing and approval.

In Memphis, during that time, minors were not allowed to get married, even with parental consent. They found where they could get married. Elmer borrowed a friend's old car while Mama kept the baby and headed out of state to Arkansas. During their road trip that old car had at least twenty flat tires. Every mile or two they would have to stop and pull over for Elmer to fix a flat tire. Each tire got a flat at least four times. They thought that they would never get to Arkansas, or get married. Finally, they arrived with the proper documents, including Mary's letter of consent. The young couple was married on August 15, 1941. Their car was so unreliable, Selena and Elmer prayed all the way back to Memphis, Tennessee.

Praise God, they made it back without another flat tire. Elmer immediately began thinking of a better way to provide a better living for his new family. He heard jobs were plentiful with better wages up north in Chicago, Illinois. Mary's older sister, Lucy and her husband, Mr. Y.T., had recently moved there from Memphis after staying with Mary and her four children long enough to save some traveling money. In fact, they had shared Selena's room. Lucy and Mr. Y. T. seemed pleased with the new big city. They found an apartment on 38th and State up over a little grocery store.

Aunt Lucy wrote back and told her sister, Mary, about Chicago and the jobs that she and Y.T. acquired. Y.T. was hired at the stock yard and Lucy got a job cooking and cleaning for a white family on the north side of Chicago. Many other southerners were migrating north to Chicago, Detroit, and even St. Louis during this time. A better life, better jobs and more money was the buzz circulating in the south. For those that had the nerve, they stepped out on faith and seized the opportunity of what they hoped would be a better way of living.

As young as Elmer was, he was intrigued by the talk of the big city life. To that end, he saved enough change to get a one-way bus ticket to Chicago. Young Elmer told his new young wife that he wanted to go to Chicago to look for a better job and that he would send for her and the baby once he found one. After the young couple shared the news with Mama, Mary wrote and asked her sister, Lucy, would it be all right if Elmer came up there and stayed with her and Y.T. while he looked for a job. Lucy agreed; she said that he and Selena were both welcome to come. Mary explained that it was no need for Selena and the baby to come until Elmer found a job. Besides, he only had enough money to buy one bus ticket for now.

After securing one last week of wages, which was very little, from working at the drugstore so he could have something in his pocket, Elmer was ready to go. Mama helped Selena fix him some food for traveling, which included a couple of biscuits and salt pork. Elmer kissed and hugged Selena, then hugged the family goodbye before going to get in his friend's car. Paul rode with the friend to take Elmer to the bus station. Paul and Elmer's friend shook Elmer's hand, hugged him with brotherly love and wished him luck. And his story, like so many others, was just a small part of what made up what was to become the Great African American Migration from the South to the North.

Elmer was the youngest boy in his family. His father and other siblings were scattered mostly in Memphis, too, but he did let them know that he was leaving, even though he spent most of his time with the Green family. Elmer arrived in Chicago and made it to Aunt Lucy and Mr. Y.T.'s apartment.

Lucy had cooked some black-eyed peas with salt pork, sweet potatoes and corn bread. Elmer was glad to get there and he enjoyed the meal that they welcomed him to.

The next morning, Elmer set out to look for a job. With his enthusiasm, it did not take him long. In about two weeks after traveling all over the city, he went to the north side of Chicago and was hired by Mr. Inswiley to park cars in a garage. Elmer was an excellent driver. In fact, he was good at several things. He could box and he could play some baseball; he played excellent shortstop. Elmer's driving skills combined with his exciting energetic actions were just what his new boss was looking for. Elmer didn't miss work and he was always on time. He passed all of the unspoken tests that his new boss was leery of. Mr. Inswiley liked him and grew to trust him.

He paid him $35.00 a week, and he earned tips from the residents of the building. Elmer was happy and proud of himself. After giving Aunt Lucy money for room and board and food, (mainly supper,) he was able to save enough money to send for his wife and baby.

Selena packed her and the baby's few clothing items in her one small suitcase. Mama didn't have much, but she gave her little girl one of her granite pans to cook in. Big Aunt (pronounced Big Ain't), who was her mother's Aunt Mary and whom she was named after, had made Selena a pretty blue quilt. Big Aunt had heard it was cold up there in the windy city and hoped that this quilt would add some comfort to her niece. She felt that, with the patchwork quilt, her little niece would always have a piece of home and family.

Nevertheless, Selena's mother was worried and scared about her daughter, with her being so young and so far away from her. She did everything she could and told her everything she could think of, especially how to help her Aunt Lucy anyway she could and to be respectful and appreciative.

Mary's friend, Mr. Fred, drove Mary, Selena and the baby to the bus station. Mary was sad as she kissed her first baby girl goodbye and said another prayer for her daughter and her new little family as she held her daughter and the grandbaby close. Mary prayed all the time at least twice a day for her entire family, as well as herself, but this week called for heavy prayer with baby girl getting ready to start a new a life so far away.

One thing that kind of eased her mind was that she cut Selena's fingernails while she lie in bed asleep one night to make sure that she would not accidently scratch the baby. Selena was a little upset when she woke up and saw that her mother cut her fingernails, but she knew better than to act to disturbed because Mama did not play. In fact, she told Selena to keep them cut for the baby's safety.

After getting Selena and the baby on the bus, Mary returned home, went into her room, buried herself in her bed and cried her heart out from the depths of her soul. Her continuous sobbing frightened her younger daughters, Earline and Eileen. They ran over to Ms. Mabel's and told her that their mother would not stop crying. Miss Mabel rushed over and ran into Mary's room.

"Mary, what you cryin' for?"

Mary sobbed, "My little girl done left, gone all the way to Chicago and she got that little baby." She cried some more. "She don't know how to take care of no baby."

"Mary, she gone be all right. The Good Lord takes care of all of his children." She continued, "Stop that crying. You don't want to make yourself sick, do you? She and the baby will be just fine."

Chapter Eleven

❦

Selena was a little afraid of leaving Mama and everything she knew to be home. However, it was comforting to know that Elmer was there, waiting for her. At the same time, she was also grateful to have one of her elders, her Aunt Lucy, there to welcome her, as well. The slight fear and anxiety that she had were combined with excitement and hope.

Selena recalled that she had never been as cold as she was on that bus. It was freezing on that bus, and to top it off, just before the bus arrived in Chicago, she became sick to her stomach. The bus driver had to stop the bus somewhere close to Chicago, maybe Kankakee, to let Selena off to throw up. It probably was her nerves and a bit of motion sickness that caused her to become ill.

A lady passenger was kind enough to hold the baby while Selena got off the bus to regurgitate. Selena felt better after that. She boarded the bus again and the bus continued on its journey to Chicago.

Lucy and Mr. Y.T. still owned their Oldsmobile that they had driven from Memphis to Chicago and were able to drive Elmer to the bus station to pick Selena and the baby up when she arrived.

Elmer and Selena were ecstatic to see each other, and both her Aunt Lucy and Y.T were happy to see Selena. Y.T. got behind the wheel, everyone else piled in the car and they headed back to Lucy's apartment on 38th Street. Lucy had prepared Great

Northern beans, baked sweet potatoes and corn bread for supper. Elmer put what little belongings Selena had brought away while Selena fed the baby. Once the baby was fed and had been burped, Selena and Elmer joined Aunt Lucy and Mr. Y.T. in the kitchen for that delicious supper that smelled so good. They each topped it off with a cold glass of buttermilk, which made Selena feel right at home.

Aunt Lucy was always a great cook; her food was always delicious. She loved to cook her own food, even when she was sick, while Selena and her family were still living there. Aunt Lucy would sit at the kitchen table and Selena would hand her everything she needed for that meal, from the right ingredients to the right pot or pan that Aunt Lucy wanted to use. Although Selena offered to cook, Aunt Lucy wanted to cook it herself. Selena remained her assistant as she watched and learned just as she had when watching her mother cook back home. It paid off; Selena became an excellent cook.

About three months had passed and Aunt Lucy's attitude began to change. Let's face it. She became downright mean. It was evident that she was tired of her house guests. She had forgotten the fact that in Memphis, she and Mr. Y.T. had been house guests to Mary and her children. She had slept in Selena's room for a longer time than Selena had been staying in her apartment.

One of the issues was just a natural part of development. Selena and Elmer's baby had learned how to walk at six months, and as babies do, she became adventurous.

Aunt Lucy had a few trinkets on her cocktail table that she was adamant that she did not want the baby to touch. Selena made sure to watch the baby to insure that she did not touch anything. Even when the baby forgot, Selena hit her hand and told her, "No." After that, the baby never forgot. She never touched the table, let alone the trinkets on it again. The baby had been using the table to keep her balance when she wasn't holding on to her mother, Selena.

Aunt Lucy wouldn't have that to complain about anymore. Somehow, the baby kept her balance, learned to walk better and faster with Selena's help, but without touching that table. That wasn't enough, though. Aunt Lucy started picking on Selena for any and everything. Nothing Selena did satisfied her aunt. Lucy even wrote a letter to Mary, talking about how awful Selena was, writing that Selena was as crazy as a Switch engine. She even asked Mary how she dealt with her. Fortunately, Mary knew her daughter and she knew her sister real well. Though she loved them both, she didn't want to rush to judgment.

Therefore, she wrote a letter to Selena telling her what Lucy wrote and asked Selena what had happened.

All of the lies that Lucy had told surprised and sincerely hurt Selena. She wrote her mother back, explaining how she had been on her best behavior and did everything that Aunt Lucy had asked her to do, most of the time, before she even asked her to do it. She related how she took it upon herself to keep the house clean. In fact, she didn't let Aunt Lucy do anything, except cook because she insisted. Selena went on to explain that as soon as Aunt Lucy was finished with a dish or a pot, she would wash it, dry it and put it away, trying to make everything easier on her aunt. Mary believed her daughter and she knew that her sister had a mean streak in her.

Mary told her daughter maybe it was time for her and Elmer to look for a place of their own, but to try to stay out of Lucy's way as much as possible until they could get moved.

Despite all of Selena's efforts, Lucy had been so mean to Selena, Mr. Y.T. asked Lucy what was wrong. Lucy cussed him out and told him to mind his own damn business. He shook his head in disbelief and never spoke on it again. Besides, Mr. Y.T. enjoyed their company, especially having Elmer to talk baseball and boxing with. He enjoyed playing with the baby. He saw how nice and clean Selena kept the house and the little money that they were paying them was a help, too.

Selena had been in her and Elmer's room with the baby reading that letter over and over with tear stained eyes when he came in from work. Elmer wondered what was wrong with her. Selena showed him the letter from Mama filled with all of those lies. Elmer wanted to confront Aunt Lucy to ask her why would she say those awful, untrue things about Selena. However, Selena would not allow him to confront her. Instead, she told him that they had to find their own place to live and they needed to find it soon.

After that, Elmer brought a paper home with him every day after work. Together, he and Selena would look for some place affordable after eating supper.

Finally, they found a place. Together, the two of them decided that Elmer would go and see the place immediately after work. Elmer made an appointment to see the place on 60th and May. He informed the landlord that he worked on the north side and because of the snow, it may take a while to get there. The landlord offered to wait.

When Elmer arrived, he found that the apartment was a small place with a kitchen, bathroom and one middle room. Elmer thought it was good enough for a start. There was one problem that would burst Elmer's bubble. The man did not want any children in his building. Not only did they have one toddler, but they were now expecting their second child. Elmer left with his head hung, but not for long.

If Elmer didn't have anything else he had pride. If the man did not want him and his family there, he did not want to be there. Elmer walked backed to the carline (that's what they called the bus stop back then) and took the bus back to Aunt Lucy's apartment. When he arrived, Selena noticed the disappointment in his face and followed him to their room where they could talk privately. Elmer informed her that they could not get it.

Selena asked him why not. He kept saying, "We can't get that one. We'll just have to keep looking—that's all." After Selena's persistence, Elmer told her that the man did not want to rent to people with children. Selena told Elmer to give her the paper with the man's address on it.

"Didn't you hear what I said?" he asked her,

"The man say he don't want no children."

Selena, continuing to put on her boots, determined not to accept "no" as the final word, and more determined to get out of her aunt's house. She grabbed her coat and the paper and trudged through the deep snow to the carline. Selena was big and pregnant and still kind of new to the city, but she did not let that stop her.

She didn't even let Elmer calling her a smart alleck in an effort to deter her from her mission. First of all, she could read, and with God's guidance, she found the place. She introduced herself to the landlord, and found out he was serious about not wanting children in the building, or so he thought. Selena opened up with her most humble tone of voice.

"My husband told me that you did not want children in your building, but I promise you that nothing will happen to your property. We have one little girl, still a baby.

"Mister Barker, I promise you we will take good care of your apartment. And it will be kept clean."

Mr. Barker's heart softened a bit and he admired her determination. He thought to himself this young girl had the nerve to come all the way here in the deep snow, several months pregnant after I told her husband no had to have guts. Selena, not sure which way or what he was thinking, broke the silence.

"Mr. Barker, we really need this apartment. We live with my aunt and we really need to move."

"Okay, okay, you got it," he responded. "How much furniture do you have?"

"We ain't got no furniture. We ain't got nothing, sir".

Mr. Barker showed her a card table that he had stored in his basement and asked her if she wanted it…she did. After Mr. Barker brought the table up to their new apartment and cleaned it off they shook hands.

Selena smiled all the way back to Aunt Lucy's. She was so happy that she hadn't noticed that her feet were numb from the cold and snow until she made it back home to share the good news with Elmer.

Her feet were frost bitten. Elmer was shocked and a little upset; actually his ego was bruised. He did not like that his wife had accomplished something that he hadn't. It would be a long time, many years before he realized that as long as two people who want the same thing and are reaching for the same goal are together, it does not matter who pulls the winning pull in this tug of war called life, as long as you're on the same team.

Right away Selena and Elmer packed their bags and moved that Saturday so that Elmer would not have to miss a day of pay. Elmer wondered how Selena persuaded that white man to change his mind. He asked her, "What did you say to him?"

"I promised him that none of us would mess up his property and told him we really had to move from where we were staying," Selena answered.

"He is a nice man. He gave us a table after I told him we didn't have anything to move."

As mean as Aunt Lucy had been, she insisted that her and Mr. Y.T. drive them to their new apartment. As much as Lucy wanted them to leave, I know she was going to miss how clean her niece kept her apartment. When they arrived at Selena and Elmer's apartment, Lucy walked around, her nose squinted, searching for what was wrong with the place, instead of what was right with it. Even so, she could not find anything.

Lucy managed a weak smile and told them it was a nice place. After a while, Aunt Lucy and Mr. Y.T. decided that they would head back home now that they knew that they were in a nice place. Lucy would be able to tell her sister, Mary, that she had taken care of her baby girl and made sure she was in a nice place. Selena and Elmer thanked them both for everything and hugged them goodbye.

Selena wrote her mother about their new place and expressed her wish that her mother would come to Chicago as she had in all of her letters during the past year. Her mother was glad they had their own place now, but was still uncertain about leaving the South. When she shared the news with her son, Paul, he was willing to give Chicago a chance.

He told his mother that he would go for a visit to see how it was. Paul, Elmer and Selena were so happy to see each other, they laughed and swapped stories about what was going on in Memphis and what was happening in Chicago all night. They didn't have any beds, Selena, Elmer slept on the floor with the baby and Paul slept in the bathtub. Right away, Paul found a job and decided to stay. He really liked Chicago.

Once Mama heard that Paul wasn't ready to come home and had found a job, too, she thought maybe there was hope for her and her two younger children. The fact that she missed Selena and the baby nudged her even more, but what was most important to her was for her and all of her children to be in the same town. She loved all four of them and wanted to be near all of them. Selena kept praying and hoping that Mama would change her mind and decide to come and be with her. Selena always knew and felt in her heart.

"If Mama comes, or when Mama comes, everything will be all right," Selena would say. They loved each other; her mother was her best friend. After calling on the name of The Lord, Mama was the next name Selena would call and, just like the Lord, her mother never let her down.

Chapter Twelve

Soon after Paul came, Elmer's father, Mr. Parker, came from the South, looking for a better life for himself. Mr. Parker was upset to see Selena sleeping on the floor, especially being pregnant. He told her that her baby would grow to her, sleeping on the floor.

That frightened her to the point of tears. Selena was crying so hard it unnerved Elmer. He was livid that his father told her that. "Why did you tell her that?" Elmer questioned his father. But that same day, Elmer, his dad and Paul went walking through the alleys, looking for anything that Selena could sleep on.

They found an old mattress and brought it back and laid it on the floor of the room Selena had been sleeping in. Selena and the baby slept at the top of the mattress and out of respect and concern for his aging father, Elmer let his father sleep at the foot of the mattress. He continued to sleep on the floor.

One night just before day, Selena awoke to see Mr. Parker sitting in the window. She asked him why he wasn't laying down.

"Any man, woman or child sleep in that bed is subject to a paralysis stroke," Mr. Parker stated with sincere despair, but the way he sounded when he said it, provoked hysterical laughter through their little apartment. Paul even laughed his way out of the bathtub.

The truth be told, none of them were comfortable; I guess that is what made it so funny to all of them. All of them laughed so hard and made so much noise that their neighbor came upstairs and asked them would they please keep it down because he had a sick relative in his apartment. They could hardly stop laughing, but they were mindful to keep it way down out of respect and consideration for the sick neighbor.

The next morning, Elmer and Paul went to work while Mr. Parker stayed home with Selena and read his Bible. Selena took care of her baby girl, cleaned the little apartment and began making preparations to cook supper. Selena had one granite speckled pan; she cooked everything in that one pan. If she cooked beans, she would cook them first, put them in the plates and sit them on the stove to keep warm while she washed out the pan so she could make the bread or whatever else she would cook to go with the meal. It wasn't easy, but she always thanked God that everything was as good as it was, because she knew that there were others who had it so much harder.

Selena never stopped praying and longing for her mother to come.

Selena went about her daily routine, but this day turned out to be different. She opened her weekly letter from her mother.

"Mama's coming, Mama's coming! Everything is gone be fine," she screamed. It was warmer now; summer had just ended. Selena was glad of that. She did not want the winter weather to frighten her mother.

It was September, 1942. Elmer and Paul went to the bus station to meet Mama and the girls. Mary was upset; her first day in Chicago was a chilling horror. She and the girls were extremely cold. Fall hadn't even begun; but guess what happened? IT SNOWED!!! Mary threatened to go back home to Memphis. Selena, Elmer and Paul did their best make sure Mary and the girls were warm and comfortable.

Once she looked around, able to see all four of her children at one time, she finally warmed up. She was too happy to see her eldest daughter and only son to go back to Memphis, anyhow.

As a family, they all pulled together. Selena watched her two younger sisters while Mama went to work at the Campbell Soup company. It was pretty decent she made about $18.00 a week. They all potted their money together to save for a bigger place.

It was an English basement on 36th and Giles, but it was much more room than they had on 60th and May, but it cost more. There were times when money was so tight that Paul would take his little niece outside with him and stand. Because she was such a cute baby girl, people would give her enough pennies and nickels that Paul was able to treat the family to hamburgers.

The family made the best of their new place and thanked God that they were able to be together in the same city. One night Elmer was on his way home from work and two men approached him and asked him for a light.

He made a motion toward his pocket and cold cocked one of the guys and did a swift upper cut on the other one. He whipped the two of them so fast they were crawling away from him. They had picked the wrong one to try to stick up that night. Elmer was a prize fighter. He would fight at the neighborhood gym and he would win. He earned a little extra money doing that after work sometimes.

A worst tragedy occurred one night under the el not far from their apartment. One evening, a lady was gang raped by a group of boys, when she was on her way home. That was terrible news, but it got worst. The boys were laughing as they held her down and took turns. When the last boy was ready for his turn, he had gotten on top of her and just before he invaded her, he looked in her face. It was his own dear mother. The news spread that he jumped up and went into shock. It was said that he lost his complete mind and never got it back. That is something to think about on so many levels.

First of all, God's law states, "Vengeance is mine saith The Lord." No form of man-made punishment could have hurt or tormented that boy the way his own mind and memory did. Also when you set out to hurt others in any way, the person may not be your mother and may not be a mother at all; perhaps, she's somebody's sister or aunt, or he's somebody's brother or uncle. One thing for certain, it's somebody's child, someone's loved one.

Chapter Thirteen

The family heard about some new project apartments being built on Chicago's west side near Roosevelt, (at the time known as "Jew town"). They were interested in moving there so they inquired and found out that it would be almost a year before they were ready for occupancy. However, applications were being taken for potential tenants.

Selena and Elmer filled out an application for an apartment. Mama filled out a separate application for her and her two younger daughters to occupy. In case one of the applications were approved and the other was not they would still be in. Now all they could do was wait for approval.

Thanksgiving was coming and so was Selena's and Elmer's new baby. Selena and Mama were in the kitchen together two days before the big eating day, preparing a Thanksgiving feast; they had been saving left over cornbread and biscuits from the past week to go with the fresh baked cornbread for the dressing. Mary had picked and cleaned the mixed greens (mustard, turnips and spinach) baked sweet potato pies and a peach cobbler. Selena baked the cakes, Chocolate, Jelly, Caramel and Coconut.

That baby must have smelled all of that good cooking going on and wanted out. There was no time between Selena putting the finishing touch of icing on the Caramel cake and her first labor pain stopped her where she stood. Before she knew it, Selena was doubled over in labor. Elmer helped Selena into a taxi and went straight to the County hospital. Mama stayed at home with her two younger children and her oldest granddaughter. Paul came in and waited with his mother to hear the news from Elmer.

Elmer and Selena were happy about the successful birth of their second child; a beautiful baby girl. She was gorgeous; she had her father's widow's peak, her mother's cheek bones, her grandmother's reddish brown, sandy-colored hair and the most beautiful hazel eyes. They named her Juanita; she was often called by her nickname, Ni-Ni, pronounced Nee-Nee. Juanita was a pretty, tiny baby.

Mama had finished preparing Thanksgiving dinner for the family while Selena was recuperating in the hospital. Mama had put Selena up a plate with some of everything they had on their menu on it for when she was released from the hospital. After the family's prayer of thanks, Elmer sliced the turkey and Paul sliced the ham. Mama fixed the children's plates first. The grown folks went for themselves, dishing up a bit of everything; turkey, dressing, potato salad, greens, and macaroni with cheese, cranberry sauce and so on; you know the drill.

Two days after Thanksgiving, Elmer picked Selena and their new baby girl up from the county hospital in a taxi. Mary had stayed home from work to see her two youngest children off to school and take care of Selena and Elmer's oldest baby girl. By the time Selena and little Juanita were released from the hospital and taken home, her younger sisters were home from school. The family gathered around Selena to get a glimpse of the new baby. Paul congratulated his brother-in law and sister as he joined in on the baby talk.

Mama had taken her new grandbaby to her "like new" bassinet with clean fresh linen in it; all of which the family had pooled together to buy from their favorite resell store.

Selena recuperated and returned to being the daily caregiver for her two children and her two sisters while Mary and Elmer went to work. Selena would comb her sisters' hair for school every day, bathe and dress her daughters, wash diapers and clean the apartment, prepare breakfast and lunch for everyone. Sometimes, if Selena didn't get around to cooking supper, Mary would cook when she got in from work. On weekends, Mary would always cook the meals and help with the family laundry.

Shortly thereafter, Selena and Mama found a church that they both loved. They took the four little ones with them every Sunday. Progressive Baptist Church was their new church home, built at its first location before the city wanted to put in that new expressway; the Dan Ryan. The family loved the service, the pastor could preach, the choir could sing, the church itself was beautiful, and it wasn't far from their home.

Paul attended church sometimes, way more than Elmer, who rarely attended. The first time he attended, the Pastor asked Elmer to take up the offering. His anger due to his acute shyness made him swear that he wasn't going anymore. Paul was a Baptist Training Union instructor and had been reared in the church all of his life.

Elmer saw his father carry the Bible every day, but he was a negative example to him, mainly because of the way Mr. Parker had allowed Elmer's stepmother to mistreat him and his other remaining siblings when they were children. Mostly, Elmer hated how his stepmother would lie to and cheat on his father.

In the meantime, Paul married his first wife, Ernestine. She was a pretty woman with a pleasant personality. The family loved her. Ernestine lived on the Westside and had one son; Paul moved in with her, once they married. Paul and Ernestine would join Mama and Selena often.

Even when they didn't go to church, they would join the family for Sunday dinner. Ernestine was a good cook, but Paul had cooking skills, too; after all, he was Mary's son. The two newlyweds would often bring Ernestine's son and a dish or two to add to the dinner.

Winter was almost over when Selena, Elmer and Mama Mary received their letters of response concerning the applications that they filled out for the new projects on the Westside. "Mr. & Mrs. Elmer Parker you are approved as tenants for the newly built Robert Brooks homes. If you are still interested we will need to hear from you within thirty days to secure your occupancy request." Selena and Elmer's letter read; Mary's read the same, except it was addressed to Mrs. Mary Green. Selena and Mama Mary checked the appropriate boxes on their separate letters, signed them and put them in the mail that evening.

They wanted to make sure that they were way in front of the deadline because they definitely wanted to move into the newly built homes. The three heads of the household were thrilled to receive notification that they could come to the office of Robert Brooks's homes to sign the lease agreement and look over their assigned units. Selena and her mother took the bus to the new housing project. They both loved their own assigned unit and each other's.

Selena and Elmer had a two bedroom, ground floor unit at 1358 W. 14th Street. Mary's unit for her and her two younger daughters was a one bedroom, second floor corner unit at 1391a Loomis. Though she and Henry were not divorced as of yet, they remained separated. He was still in Mississippi so the one bedroom was fine for her and her daughters. Selena and Mary walked back to the car line, gleaming with excitement over how they were going to love their new places.

Selena, Mama and Elmer began packing their little belongings in preparation for the move. Elmer asked a friend from work, who had a car, if he could help him and the family move. Lucy and Mr. Y.T. helped them move with their Oldsmobile. Paul helped, too. Once the families were settled in their new places, they went looking for beds and linen at the resell shop on Canal. The store had used furniture and goods; some were from private citizens and some were from hotels that were either remodeling and updating their establishments or closing them.

Whatever the circumstances, the merchandise was always decent and usually very nice. The owner was a nice family man, willing to work with his customers. He came to know the matriarch, Mary, Selena and their family very well. He gave them his trust and offered them the privilege of paying on time and they did not abuse that trust. That was the beginning of a lifetime relationship between the business owner and Mary's family for decades to come.

Mary's big four poster bed with dresser and mirror to match were delivered within two days to her place. Mary and her two little girls shared that bed. Selena and Elmer, having the two bedrooms, bought a bed for the baby girls to share in their room and a bed for themselves; they were delivered right after Mary's. There was a block in between Mother and daughter now, but it did not matter because they saw each other every day. Selena still watched over her sisters while their mother worked and combed their hair for school. After school, they would return to their big sister's house until Mama came from work.

Now that the family had moved to the Westside, Paul and Ernestine would visit more often. They were having lovers' quarrels quite often; if Ernestine wasn't putting Paul out, he was leaving. One day, Mary was tired of their bickering, and out of love for the both of them, went to their house while they were still sleep and tied them together by their feet and waited for them to wake up. Once they were awake and tried to get up, they realized that they were hooked together.

Mary spoke her mind once they calmed down and realized that they could not go anywhere. She advised them with as much love and wisdom as she could. The three of them had a good laugh and she finally untied them after they agreed to try to get along better and stop all of that foolishness.

Chapter Fourteen

More and more tenants were moving in, making lifelong friendships and kinships. Selena and Elmer's next door neighbor's last name was Green, just like Selena's mother and father's. In fact, Selena's father and the neighbor next door were both named Henry Green. Emma and Henry Green who were closer to Selena's parents' age lived next door to Selena and Elmer Parker with their pretty daughter.

Ms. Emma Green missed having a baby around because her daughter was almost grown, a teenager like Selena, but still at home with her parents. Ms. Emma Green took over Selena and Elmer's baby girl, Juanita. She absolutely loved her. Juanita was so little and cute Ms. Emma would say. Ms. Emma would come over to the Parkers to visit and hold Juanita. If Selena needed to go the store or anything, Ms. Emma didn't need a reason or excuse. She wanted Juanita with her. She would take her to her own house or she would hold and cuddle her right there in Selena and Elmer's house.

It had been a while, but Paul and his wife were on shaky ground again. This time it was serious. Someone new, younger and prettier had put a twinkle in Paul's eye. It was the next door neighbor's Henry and Emma's daughter. That girl was the only apple of her parents' eyes for so long that she was certain that the world felt that way about her. Once she displayed her feelings of affection toward Paul, who was a little older than her, she was sure he would not be able to resist. Her parents liked Paul, but not only was he older than their daughter, but most importantly he was married. However, she was a swift girl and her parents couldn't tell her anything. Emma and her husband Henry had met Paul's wife and they liked her.

Selena and Mary felt real bad about Paul spending so much time with the neighbor's daughter even though they did like the girl they liked Ernestine a lot. Selena and Mary's bad feelings turned to sadness when Paul announced he was divorcing his wife to marry his new love.

Selena's new sister-in-law was so nice, friendly and full of fun that the two of them became very close friends. Paul and his bride stayed next door with her parents, his new in-laws. The two newlyweds would often walk next door to Selena and Elmer's to play cards and have fun.

Selena kept her sisters' hair, her two little girls' hair, and her mother's hair, as well as her own hair, looking so good that the neighbors asked her if she would do theirs. She became the kitchen beautician; doing hair in her pantry. Charging 15 cents a head, Selena started washing and combing hair. Soon she was able to buy a pressing comb and one pair of Marcel irons. Her fee went up to fifty cents a head. Selena loved doing hair and the money was a help to her and her family. She felt good about herself. She was asked to join social clubs; she even helped form one. It was fun for a while until it came time for their party. The treasurer didn't have the dues money that she had been trusted to keep.

She kept making excuses; she promised she would have the money within a couple of weeks. The treasurer had stolen all of the club members' money and bought new furniture. Selena and her brother, Paul, who was the sweetheart of the social club, sat outside of the treasurer's house all day on the day she promised to pay. No one knew how the lady came up with the money, but she did; she paid it back. Of course, she was dismissed from the club after that.

Selena was enjoying the art of hair so much she decided to go to beauty school. She figured she'd learn more about her craft and make more money doing it. After achieving and receiving her GED, Selena enrolled in the Madame C.J. Walker School of beauty culture, which was located on the south side of Chicago on 47th street. By this time her father, Henry, arrived in Chicago. Elmer helped Henry secure a job close to his in a smoked fish house.

Henry slept on Selena and Elmer's couch, and he would babysit his grandchildren when he was not working. Selena would not be far, maybe gone to the store, unless she was at school; which she attended part-time.

One day Selena was home with her children, cleaning the house and took it upon herself to move the refrigerator. A sharp pain went through her side and she had to go to the doctor. After Elmer, Henry and Mary all came home from work, Elmer took Selena to the doctor for an examination. Mary cooked dinner at her house and invited Henry to bring their grandchildren with him to eat.

Selena thought that she had pulled a muscle or something. She strained her back and side. She also discovered she was several months pregnant with their third child. The doctor restricted her to bed rest for two weeks and scheduled a follow up appointment. Selena was discouraged and disappointed; it seemed to her that every time she thought she had something to look forward to, she ended up pregnant. This time it was beauty school; she would have to stop going.

Five months later, she gave birth to a handsome sandy head baby boy. Elmer Parker Jr. was named after his father. He, too, had his father's widow's peak and his father's hands with a perfect blend of both his mother and father's facial features; he was very cute. Mary's first grandson warranted lots of attention. He was a sweet baby and the first boy born in the family since his uncle Paul was born. Paul and his wife had even had a pretty baby girl two years younger than little Juanita and two years older than her new cousin, Elmer Jr. Elmer was happy to have a son and thrilled that he was his namesake.

After bonding with her son for about a year, Selena wanted to return to beauty school. Still doing hair in her kitchen pantry, Selena would talk about going back to school to get her license. Family and friends encouraged her to do so.

By this time, Elmer had joined some of his older brothers' habits of drinking. He became more argumentative towards everyone, especially his wife, Selena. He didn't even want her going to the store; he wanted her to stop participating in the social club she was in. One time Selena was getting dressed for a dance that the club was hosting; it was during the time of the hit movie "Carmen Jones." The fashion trend was the "Carmen Jones" skirt. All of the ladies who could afford it, were buying them or making them; whether they looked good on them or not. Selena was able to purchase one and she looked fab-u-lous in it.

In fact, it looked so good on her that Elmer promised to buy her ten more skirts, if she just would not wear that one. Selena loved herself in that skirt; the way it wrapped around her small waistline and draped over her hypnotic hips.

There was no way she was taking that skirt off. Elmer was so angry he refused to go to the party with her. She went anyway and had a nice time. When she returned home, Elmer had locked her out of the house and would not let her in. Selena, shocked that she could not get into her own house, regrouped and spoke out loud. "That's okay. I know where I can go stay."

Elmer flung the door open and she was able to go in. He stayed angry a day or two longer. To Selena that began to be normal because he was always angry and arguing about something since he began drinking. He would come in, open the refrigerator and slam it, looking for something to eat, if he didn't have a taste for what had been cooked. Elmer had gotten so mean that the neighbors, who would be visiting with Selena while she cooked or dressed hair, would hear his footsteps coming up the walkway and run out of there.

Ms. Emma would say, "Here come that little evil man."

Elmer was a short man in statue, but he was no play toy. He was a man's man, a powerhouse when he got mad. People did not mess with him. They respected him and so did their children. There were times when he was his true self, nice, kind and full of fun.

Selena and Elmer were the first tenants in their project to own a television set. Elmer bought a beautiful blonde-colored wood finished TV for their living room. It was exciting for the entire family. Selena had been listening to her soap operas on their transistor radio, but this was a whole new world, a new visual experience.

I wonder which was more exciting; the first time when they saw inside toilets that flushed, instead of the outhouse in the woods behind their house in the south, or the revolutionized technology of the talking picture box. Selena was now able to see her soap operas on TV. Elmer would watch some things, but when baseball season came around, the TV stayed on baseball, whenever he was in the house. Selena didn't mind. She liked baseball herself; she had been a tomboy and enjoyed playing ball and other sport games with her brother, Paul, when they were children. The children, especially the girls grew bored of baseball and began to resent it. It was on day and night.

Elmer played baseball on a local team in the area and his reputation from playing in the Negro league in Memphis traveled all the way to California. One of the teams heard about his skills and sent him a round trip ticket to come and try out for the team. He made it. This was the chance for their family to move up a little higher. Elmer had the chance to make more money, doing what he truly loved. The team officials sent him back home to share the good news with his wife and family. Everyone was thrilled, especially Selena; she encouraged him to go and pursue his love of baseball.

It was decided. He had his ticket, his wife was in agreement and the other family members assured that they would help Selena in whatever capacity that she needed. Elmer kissed and hugged his wife and children goodbye, then proceeded to the train station. Before he boarded the train, he called back home to talk to Selena. She was shocked it was him, but she didn't like how he was questioning her and he had just left. He wanted to know what she was doing; he was extremely jealous. She exclaimed that she was there with kids as she always was, just like she was when he left the house.

She was knocked off of her feet an hour later by Elmer's return home. He said he could not leave his family. He did not want to travel that far away from his family for that length of time. His mind was set; Selena was so upset with him she did not speak to him for a week.

Defeated by Elmer's fear of being too far from the family; Selena turned back to her dreams one of which was becoming a licensed beautician, servicing lots of customers. Another dream of hers was for Elmer to own his own service station and mechanic shop. He loved working on cars and making extra money repairing them, but he had no interest in opening a business.

I think because he couldn't imagine how he could ever open a business, as difficult as it was for him to provide for his family, it was easier for him to act as though he did not want a business of his own. It was easier not to dream, at least not to put any stock of hope into a dream.

On the other hand, Selena did not allow his inhibitions to hinder her dreams, though. She re-enrolled in Madame C.J. Walker's School of Beauty Culture and, in her spare time, she taught her father how to spell and write his name. In the past, he had always made his mark with an X. Afterwards, Henry was proud of being able to recognize, spell and write his own name.

Selena had help with the children while she attended beauty school. Henry, Selena's favorite brother-in-law, Perry, and her neighbor, Margaret, took turns babysitting. Margaret was Elmer Junior's godmother. It was her joy to take care of him. She adored him as much as Ms. Emma adored little Juanita. As always Selena and Elmer continued to dote over their oldest child Dee-Dee. Margaret had a daughter who played with Selena's two daughters when the three of them were home from school.

Selena's three children loved their grandfather and he loved them. All of Henry and Mary's grandchildren by Selena and Paul called Henry, "Daddy," and Mary, "Mama." That's what the children heard their parents call them and their parents were still so young, they didn't feel the need to force them to call their parents, "Grandma" and "Grandpa." The children called their own parents by their names, but they were well aware of who their parents were. However, they knew Mama and Daddy were

Mama and Daddy to everyone. Everybody listened when Mama and Daddy spoke. It was love honor and respect for them as elders and as heads of the family.

Chapter Fifteen

Perry was not only Selena's nicest and favorite brother-in-law, he was her children's favorite uncle. They would have a good time with their uncle Perry. Perry would make his nieces and nephew hot chocolate, which they loved until they saw him dip his toast into it. The children frowned in disgust at the sight of Perry taking a bite of the freshly dipped toast.

Perry laughed at their response. He told them how good it was and convinced them to try it for themselves. Surprisingly to them, they loved it and that habit has been passed down to the other descendants who never had the pleasure of meeting Perry. Perry would often tell his brother, "Elmer, you should take your wife out sometimes. Take her to the show or dinner sometimes."

Sometimes he would listen and nod; other times Elmer would wave his hand in dismissal at Perry.

Perry would simply respond, "One day you might be sorry, man."

Selena was very grateful for her three babysitters though; she always says if it weren't for them, she would not have been able to finish beauty school. Selena enjoyed beauty school and establishing her reputation. Clients would come to the school to request her. Press and Curls were the rave; Selena could press hair so straight the teachers at the school were amazed.

The dean of the school and head instructor, Ms. Journer, would walk around observing and evaluating the students. One day, Selena witnessed her pull one of the instructors to the side and whisper, "What is that Selena is using to press with?"

Although the students were instructed to use a certain Madam C.J. Walker cream, Ms. Journer knew that Selena wasn't using the school's pressing cream. At the same time, Ms. Journer loved how straight, smooth, and shiny the hair Selena pressed looked. Ms. Journer and Selena had great admiration for each other. In addition, Selena admired and respected Ms. Journer's magnificent teaching skills, as well as her abundance of knowledge. The one good thing about their relationship was Ms. Journer recognized Selena was a natural; although she was a student, the art of hair was a God-given gift simmering in Selena's heart and soul, which was beginning to manifest. Selena's press and curls looked like a perm and the perm hadn't even been introduced yet. Perm was short for permanent relaxer back then.

Selena wasn't trying to break the rules, nor disrespect the school, but the oil she pressed with made the hair straighter and shinier. In order not to disturb the peace, but still achieve head turning results, she would mix a small amount of the pressing oil she used at home in with the school's pressing oil, which always resulted in stop and stare results that led to her being one of the most requested students in the school.

Selena's speed was also a plus; she could do three clients from start to finish in the time it would take other students in her class to complete one. Moreover, the client would not have to hold her ear. The school would offer their students extra hours for each Bud Billiken Day Parade participant's hair that the students styled. As a result, Selena did so many heads that she acquired enough hours to afford her an early graduation.

Selena continued doing her clients at home and continued to study for the state board exam. Eventually, Selena passed the state board and became a licensed cosmetologist. With this achievement, she was feeling ecstatic. The glory of her accomplishment gave her a more optimistic glimpse of what her future could be, as long as she kept her faith and continued to trust in God. She always stood firmly on her belief that GOD WILL MAKE A WAY.

Though she says she doesn't know how she afforded it, Selena took her daughters to dance class every week. She realized later it was her faith in God, exercising her faith, combined with her determination to work towards a better life for herself and her family, resulted in triumphs. Not to suggest that there were not any trials or labor pains, but her gains were worth her pain.

After work, Selena would still get the children ready, pack picnic lunches and go to the park to watch Elmer play his favorite sport, baseball, during its season. Elmer had a close friend on the team with him. The friend and his wife had no children of their own, but they enjoyed being around Elmer and Selena's children; especially the wife. She would help feed them, play games with them, take them to the bathroom; completely take over them. She was literally Selena's shadow. Selena thought she was such a nice person and so good to her children.

What could be better? Their two husbands played ball together and were best friends. Selena was happy about the friendship, especially for Elmer because the last guy he trusted as a friend, turned out to be as rotten as sour milk left in the trunk of a car for three 90 degree days of summer; but he taught Elmer and Selena a hard lesson.

Elmer had vouched for the man to get a job and cosigned for the man to finance a car. The man quit the job after paying a few notes and never paid another penny on it. When Elmer found out his check had been garnished due to him cosigning, Selena had to plead with her husband to keep him from doing something he'd regret. He wanted to kill the man. Selena pleaded and begged until she convinced him it was not worth him getting into trouble.

Even though they needed every penny that they could rake and scrape, Selena told Elmer they would make it between her press and curl money and his salary. True enough, they made it through the financial crisis. Sometimes Selena would have to borrow her children's allowance money, but she always paid it back to them; either from the next head she did, or when Elmer got his paycheck, which he brought home to her to cash and use as she saw fit. Elmer and Selena vowed never to cosign for anyone, ever.

One sunny evening, most of the team players decided to take their families to a movie. It was early and the picture had not started yet. Elmer's best friend's wife greeted Selena and the children in the lobby, Elmer was coming from work and would meet them there. Selena went into the theater to get seats; the friend guided the two older children in with her while Selena followed with her youngest child. Another teammate who was already seated yelled out to the lady with Selena's children, "Where is Parker?"

The friend yelled back in a nervous response, afraid to look back at Selena, "I don't know!"

As he studied Selena for a reaction, the teammate chuckled at her answer.

Selena thought to herself, *Why is he asking her where my husband is?*

"Where is Parker?" *What did this mean?* It did not take her long to sum up that he did it purposely for her to hear it because he knew who Selena was. In fact, he knew everything and everybody. He surely knew enough not to confuse the identities of his teammates' wives.

Selena and the friend settled the children in their seats before taking their own. Suddenly, the lady who usually talked with Selena and the children nonstop, was as quiet as an embalmed corpse; she could not look at Selena in the face the entire remainder of the evening. Selena, choosing not to ignore the signals gnawing at her heart and stomach, waited until she and the family returned home and the children were in bed to confront Elmer.

Elmer was preparing for bed when Selena picked his wallet up from the dresser and opened it. To her dismay, her suspicions were confirmed. A picture of Elmer's so-called best friend's wife fell out of it. Selena confronted him, before revealing that she had the picture. Of course, he absolutely denied it. Selena explained how the other teammate was asking his friend's wife about his whereabouts. The two of them argued back and forth a little while longer, ending up with Elmer exclaiming, "That nigga's crazy!"

"Wonder what your friend would think about this?" Selena said to Elmer as she revealed the picture of the lady.

Elmer was speechless until Selena said, "Look, I'll ask your friend myself."

"I swear, nothing is going on between me and that woman. She gave me that picture, as a friend."

"If you tell her that I have found out, I will know for sure what's been going on."

The next time they went to the park, Selena's shadow was nowhere in sight. All of a sudden, Selena looked across the ball field and saw her so-called friend sitting way away from her and the children; without so much as a glance, let alone a wave, in their direction.

Selena turned to Elmer. "You told her."

He denied it with pleading eyes, hoping she would not make a scene or approach his friend with her accusations. They moved passed it, and life returned to as normal as possible. Even so, Selena kept the picture as she concentrated more on her children and her craft and less on Elmer.

Due to his garnishment, Elmer and Selena's bills were beginning to weigh heavier than usual on them. They were still making payments on their television, as well as on their matching record player. The record player had an important role in their household since it got plenty of air time. Everyone, including the neighbors, knew when Elmer was home on the weekends.

Elmer loved music and he loved it loud. I guess that's where the rest of us got it from. We all love music and love to dance. Elmer would turn the record player on with his favorite record playing as loud as the volume could go on it and then he would open the windows and the doors. He'd let the entire project enjoy his impromptu party. The ones that chose to would holler, "Parker's home!!!" and dance out in the yard all night long.

During this period, Selena and Elmer's shortage of finances forced them to seek help from the state welfare. The welfare representative arrived at their home at the appointed time to evaluate the family. Selena offered the worker a seat in the living room. Before taking the seat the worker asked, "Where is your husband, Mrs. Parker?"

Selena pointed through the blinds at the window as she answered, "There he is, right out there."

"Oh, you have a car!" the worker snarled as she whirled around to face Selena.

"If that's what you want to call it. He's trying to get it running now."

"I don't know how that's going to work. We were not aware that you and your husband owned a car."

"That piece of junk? Do you see how old that car is?"

The worker continued to shake her head, stating that she would have to get back to Selena after discussing it with her supervisor, leaving her with no hope.

Selena's faith rose up. She knew she didn't have to take these insults. She'd always known that God was her supplier.

Without hesitation, she told the worker, "That's okay. That's okay. Don't help us." She showed the lady to the door.

Surprised at this Negro's pride-filled response, the lady left, looking as though she was certain that Selena would come crawling back. The lady left so fast that Elmer wondered what she had said, if anything. He wondered if Selena had insulted the social worker until Selena told him that the problem was the piece of junk, disguised as a car.

Taking the bus back to the south side to Progressive Baptist with the children became to taxing on Selena and Mary. To save time, they joined the Greater Mount Sinai church near their home. Selena joined the choir, Mary joined the usher board, and the younger children were in the youth and children's choirs.

Chapter Seventeen

As time went by, Church members began trusting Selena with their hair, which was a good thing. However, money was still tight. Selena had heard about this beauty shop in the Pershing Hotel on 64th and Cottage Grove where a lot of black entertainers stayed when they were in town for shows. The entertainers were not allowed to stay in any hotels in downtown Chicago, even if they had a gig there.

Selena applied for a job in the shop. There was a space available and she was hired. With all of her children in school, Selena wanted to try it for a few days a week. She was so accustomed to being home for her children and her sisters when they returned home from school, she did not want to commit to full-time hours just yet. She still liked to remain involved in her children's school. Selena was at her children's school so much, she was often mistaken for a teacher or a faculty member; whether she was there for a PTA meeting, or just a surprise visit to check on her children.

Selena remained the kitchen beautician on her days at home and worked at the shop in the Pershing on her work days. The knowledge of Selena's new job where celebrities hung out and people loving their hair do's around the house proved to be more than some neighbors could stand. One person for sure proved to be a crab in the barrel.

Without warning, Selena was summoned down to the residential office of the projects. A staff member informed her that they had received an anonymous letter from a tenant, stating that Selena was doing hair, making money in the house. She was warned that if she did not cease from doing hair in the home she would have to move.

Elmer had gone to the office with Selena; as they walked home together, Elmer, afraid of being evicted from what had been home for at least twelve years, told his wife, "I guess you won't be able to do no more hair in the house."

For a moment, Selena was speechless. She tried to think of who could be that jealous of her, trying to make things a little better for her and her family. In her eyesight, between her and Elmer's hard working efforts, they still didn't have much. Selena and Elmer never found out who informed the residential office of her doing hair in her home. Selena thought out loud. "Yeah, it was probably one of those lazy women who walk around all day in a funky bathrobe; who don't want anything better in her life and who despises anyone trying to achieve a better life for themselves."

Selena was heartbroken at the thought of having to move. She loved being close to her other family members, especially her mother. Selena loved her neighbors and her church members as well. She cherished all of the family and friend love connections that stemmed from the wonderful memories over the years. Selena always won the prettiest yard contest; she had the prettiest flower garden in the project.

Selena walked into her two-bedroom unit, which was home to her three children, whom shared one of the bedrooms, her husband and herself; still pondering over the threat of having to move. The frustration on her face was erased by determination and replaced with the strength of her faith. She opened all of the blinds and proceeded to get busy with the customers she had scheduled. In her words, "I did hair forward and backward, crossways and flat."

Within a month's time, Selena had saved enough money for a new apartment. She was able to pay for a moving truck to move her and her family to their new place, at Parkway apartments on 65th and South Park. Elmer was surprised that Selena had it all lined up; the move, the truck and the new place.

Even so, moving was sad, especially for the children. They did not want to leave their friends. They did not want to transfer from their school; Juanita, the middle child, was in the eighth grade at Medill Middle School. She really wanted to complete her last year and graduate with her lifelong friends. Mary and her two younger daughters had moved into a two-bedroom unit shortly after moving to Robert Brooks projects to be closer to the school. Now Earline and Eileen were in high school and dating.

After discovering that she could make more money doing day work for wealthy families, Mary worked as a domestic in family homes on the north side for years. Her boss liked her so much that she told her cousin about the great work Mary did in her home. The cousin fell in love with Mary's work and hired her, as well. Basically, her week was split between the two families. Though she worked for the two families, her schedule allowed her to be home more for her children and her grandchildren. Although her daughters were older, Mary worried that she would not be able to look and listen out for her grandchildren, like she was accustomed to doing, due to their move to the Southside.

After continuous prayer, Mary relaxed about the move. At least it wasn't as far of a move as when Selena left Memphis and came to Chicago without her, she reasoned.

Sadly, Perry, Selena's brother-in-law, had died in a fire, which was started by him falling asleep while smoking a cigarette in his own apartment. Selena's father, Henry, lived in an apartment in back of his job, a drive-in hamburger joint on Roosevelt road, with his current wife, Pearl, and her mother. Everyone who had used Selena and Elmer's place for refuge when they arrived in Chicago was settled in their own places now.

Finally, Selena, Elmer, and their three children were settled in their new apartment. Without delay, the children had been transferred to their new schools. Selena hoped she would like her family's new apartment in the newly-constructed apartment complex, but she did not. The place was drafty and it did not feel good in the apartment to her. As a result, she kept a cold all of the time while living there. The colds elevated to a problem with her breathing; she wanted to get out of there. Until she could find another affordable place to live, she continued on her daily routine of life, going to work and taking care of her family.

Selena's new boss appeared to be happy to have Selena as part of her staff at first, but by the appearance of her actions, she began to dislike Selena. The honeymoon period soon turned to a nightmare of dissention.

As Selena became increasingly popular, the gift of her craft and how well she pleased her customers built her clientele. While exhibiting it through her work, she combined her gift of style in how she made her clients look when she finished working with their hair. Moreover, Selena was a walking billboard for her business because she always dressed immaculately in her white starched uniform, as well as she kept her own hair well-coiffed. This made her a living magnet. People were drawn to her.

Against Elmer's wishes, Selena had learned how to drive while living on the Westside and drove to the south side to work on occasions when Elmer was home. Selena's ambition helped her to overcome many obstacles. Elmer would argue the many reasons why she did not need to drive. One day, fed up with his refusal to teach her how to drive, Selena took the keys, jumped in the car, and locked the doors until she figured out what to do first. Meantime, Elmer ran around the car, horrified, trying to persuade her to get out of the car. When she refused, he begged her to at least open the door. "I'll teach you to drive," he promised.

Selena ignored his empty promises. Burning rubber, she pulled off with a vengeance; thank God there were no cars right in front of her. As she drove, she pulled from her memory bank of watching him and others drive and finally shifted the gear into drive. Selena didn't stop the car until she reached her mother's, which was about a block or two away. After coming to the window to see who was blowing their horn, Mary was shocked.

Mary ran out of the house screaming, "What are you doing, girl? You don't know how to drive!"

Suddenly Selena remembered how her mother used to drive when they lived in the south. "Look," she responded, "I'm going to learn one way or the other, and I'd like you to teach me to drive Mama."

"Wait, wait a minute," Mary answered as she got in on the passenger side.

Finally, Selena had her first lesson, the one which Mary taught her. She learned how to parallel park. She has been driving ever since. Selena became such a good driver, her father called her a skinner because of her ability to park a car in some of the tightest spots without touching the car in front or in back of her.

One good thing about the move back to the Southside was that it was closer for Selena to get to work. By this time, she had commuted from the Westside to the Southside for work and pleasure by bus and car for quite a while. There were times, once she learned how to drive, that she would drive her children and their friends to White Castle's. At that time, the only one she was aware of was on the Southside. Other times, when she wasn't doing hair at the Pershing salon, she helped her brother, Paul, in his Bar B Q restaurant. She gave that up and concentrated on her craft after a frightening incident.

Once, her brother left her alone in the restaurant while he went to buy some ingredients to make more Cole slaw.

Three guys came in pretending to be indecisive about what they wanted before placing an order for some rib tips. Once Selena's concentration was directed toward filling the order, the thug closest to her placed a gun right at the tip of her nose.

"This is a stick up," the man growled. Gasping in shock, Selena dropped the fork filled with tips and slowly opened the register to give him what little money that was in there.

It was a small amount because it was still early in the day and they had not been open long. After the thug took the little money, he felt that it was safe for him to turn his back on the visibly shaken young lady to join his two lookout accomplices. Selena was scared, but not scared stiff, after the gun was no longer in her face. She reached under the counter for the gun that she and Paul kept hidden. Without a second thought, she aimed, cocked, and fired at the three crooks, barely missing them. They ran like track stars in a marathon, but the little lady who happened to be looking in the window when all of this terrifying drama was taking place was scared stiff; still, her eyes didn't blink.

Even when people in the area, including Paul, came to see what had happened, someone had to physically move her body away from the window and, even then, she never batted an eye. When the atmosphere got calm, Selena thanked God that she had not shot the lady or any other innocent bystander.

That incident prompted Selena to do hair full-time at Anne's Salon, in the Pershing Hotel. Her time and energy were split between honing her craft and being a good and attentive mother. Selena was working so hard and fast, she had clients requesting her to service them. Ann, the owner, began to resent Selena's winning personality and skills. Ann's attitude changed for the worst, first gradually, but after a while, it grew progressively worse. At first, Selena knew she needed to work there so she had to grin and bear it.

Ann would often approach a client in Selena's chair and ask them, "Didn't I do you before?" She would sweep around their feet in a threatening manner. The client would always respond, "No".

These were new clients, who, by word-of-mouth and through Selena's reputation, would come looking for Selena to do their hair.

One day, after working about a year for Ann, Selena was giving a lady a manicure; the lady began giving Selena some words of advice and spiritual inspiration. The first thing the lady said was to read the Eighth Chapter of Romans. She said, if she read that chapter every day, combined with her winning personality and the word of God, she would never want for anything, but more importantly, she would never have to look back.

Selena listened and received everything the lady told her and began to read the eighth chapter of Romans, along with the other scriptures that she studied on a daily basis. A new plan of perseverance was revealed to Selena; daily, she began to put her plan into action. Ann had been so mean to Selena, but she kept her composure. Even when Ann was ill for a short time, Selena would save all of the money that she owed Ann and pay her upon her return. Selena would sweep and clean the shop between clients. That's one of many rituals she passed on to me. Every time she swept, she would get a new client, and so do I.

It was an exciting time in history at the Pershing Hotel Salon and the Mansfield Hotel, which was right down the street. Not only would you see celebrities who stayed there, because they were not allowed to stay in the downtown hotels, but also the pimps, working girls (prostitutes), and boosters, kept it jumping. Sixty-third to Sixty-fifth and Cottage Grove was a hot happening spot. Even Marvin Gaye, the late R&B singer, sang a song about it. It was one of the places to be on the Southside. I say one of the places to be because 43rd Street was also happening at one time or another, as well as 47th Street. Not to mention Roosevelt Road and Madison Street on the Westside.

Chapter Seventeen

Less than six months after the lady prophesied to Selena, Selena began pulling from her spiritual bank account and working her faith muscles. Following her instincts, which said the time was right to take her leap of faith, Selena placed the order for eight gas stoves for the shop she planned to open. Yes, back then the stoves had progressed from wood to gas. Selena kept her vision to herself for a while and requested that the man at the beauty supply store only contact her at work, not at her home.

Of course, he forgot and called her home. He left the message with Elmer that the stoves she had ordered would be ready in two weeks. Elmer, who worked nights sometimes and would be home during the day, was shocked! He was so upset he immediately called Selena and began interrogating her about the phone call he had just received.

Selena couldn't debate with him while she was working. She told him it was true, but she would talk to him when she returned home. Selena, disturbed by the man not honoring her request, called him immediately. He apologized to no avail.

When Selena returned home, Elmer was waiting in fury. Selena began explaining that the bar in the Mansfield had closed and the space would be available soon and she wanted to rent it; that is why she ordered the stoves. Elmer's problem was the money being spent. He wanted to know where the money was coming from to purchase all of the equipment needed to open the shop.

Selena explained, she had been paying on the stoves, and she was offered a line of credit for the other items that she needed. Elmer was furious. To appease her husband, Selena thought if Elmer would go and look at the place with her, perhaps he could see her vision as well. When they arrived, though, he was intrigued and stunned at what she had and was accomplishing without him. Instead of being proud of her, he became afraid. His fearful, faithless and uncertain spirit did not allow him to see her vision as she saw it, but that was because God had given it to her. When God places a dream in your heart others, even your closest loved ones may not share the same enthusiasm you have.

In fact, they may not be able to visualize your dream at all. That is when you have to cowboy, well in Selena's case cowgirl up, pull up your boot straps and keep it moving, then God will give you as far as YOU can see.

Selena had, in fact, already rented the space in the Mansfield and had the men working inside turning it into a salon. They were installing the pipes for the shampoo bowls, installing the gas lines for the stoves, just really fixing it up to her specifications, as well as the city and state codes.

Elmer had mixed emotions when he saw the place with the renovations being done; but his most prevalent emotion was rage. He was furious she had done all of this without discussing it with him. Bogged down with fearful negative thoughts, yet he felt conflicted. He was slightly proud of his wife, yet, he was in a livid turmoil. His pride for his wife was over shadowed by his anger, which led to some horrible arguments. Though Selena left him still arguing in what would soon be her new salon among the working men. She returned to work at Ann's shop that day, but the arguing continued for at least a week.

In the same block, there was a barber shop. The owner was so impressed with her great work ethic, he offered to help her set up her shop. Her beautiful looks surely added enhancement to his offer; he and a lot of other gentlemen would do anything to be around her.

The House of Nelson's was the name of his barber shop. Some of Chicago's innovative barbers and hair care industry pioneers worked with and for Nelson. Nelson did all of the celebrity singers who wore a process at that time; Brook Benton, Nat King Cole, some of the Motown guys, as well as the neighborhood celebrities, who were the pimps and the pastors.

Nelson took Selena to the place to order her styling chairs. She ordered custom barber chairs. They were reclining orange leather barber chairs with cream leather piping around the edges. They had adjustable, removable headrests, which were perfect for doing eyebrow arches.

Things were falling into place. The custom ordered chairs were being made, the stoves were being held and Selena was constantly working and making money for her own shop.

Selena never spoke a word to anyone in Ann's shop about her plans to open her own salon, but her co-workers were paying close attention. When Selena got ready to leave she thanked her boss Ann, and wished her well. As much as Ann despised Selena's talent, she hated to see her leave; but she became okay with it, because she knew in her soul, that Selena's spirit was not the type to follow, but one of leadership.

Upon the completion of the renovations, Selena began making preparations to have her stoves, chairs, stools, shampoo bowls with matching chairs and manicuring table delivered to her Mansfield Hotel salon—"Selena's House of Beauty." Selena moved into the Mansfield Salon, which was beautiful; her shop was complete with new everything and mirrors everywhere.

Selena had not solicited for any operators yet, but that was the least of her worries. She knew one stylist that she could count on for sure, which was herself.

Once Selena opened her salon, operators were coming to her, asking to work in her salon; even some of her former co-workers from Anne's shop. People like new and pretty things. She dressed up her shop window so pretty and elegant that it enticed any and every observer. They all wanted to come in and become a part of it; whether they were selling something, having services rendered, or just enjoying being part of the atmosphere.

Selena attended trade shows in and out of the state. One time, she drove to a show with some of her new employees and friends who happened to be gay. Except for the rain storm that she had to drive through on the way back to Chicago, they had a ball. Donald and Henrietta were her passengers. Henrietta was so frightened that he pulled his coat over his head; but Donald was in Diva mode. He had his legs crossed; his foot arched and was taking a beauty nap. Selena hit him and told him to wake up and help her to see how to drive. He answered, "Look, you the one driving and I don't know anything about driving."

Then he asked her what she wanted him to do.

Selena shot back, "Sing, Negro!" She added, "Stay wake!"

After they burst into laughter, Henrietta included, Donald started singing.

They made it back to Chicago safely. Selena drove straight home to let Elmer know she had made it safely, but she was going to take Donald and Henrietta home and she would return shortly.

Elmer, infuriated again, asked, "What are they doing in the car and what are you doing with them?"

"These are my friends," she snapped, before pulling off.

Elmer knew who they were, because they worked in the shop…well, Donald did, but Henrietta mainly hung around the shop and brought them food and sometimes cleaned the shop. His other job was at night where he worked at a club as a shake dancer.

That was the beginning of lifelong friendships between the three of them; especially Selena and Donald. Henrietta was there a lot, but by Donald and Selena working together and him eventually becoming the manager of Selena's, they were together daily.

I recall hearing a few stories about some of the experiences they shared; both good and bad. The first challenge they experienced together was because some might say a hater meant it for bad, but God worked it for the Good by turning it into a victory, as it became one of the lessons in business that Selena never forgot.

One cold winter morning Selena received a notice requesting her presence downtown to discuss a letter that was received by the Department of Registration and education concerning one of her employees who was working without a cosmetology license. Selena took Donald with her because she knew he hadn't finished his hours. However, Selena had no idea that he had stopped completely. Selena and Donald prayed before leaving the shop, heading to their appointment.

Upon arrival, Selena and Donald listened to the letter the man read to them. Selena promised that Donald would go back to school; she would see to it. After explaining how good Donald was with hair, informing the gentleman that Donald was a natural, who was truly gifted, the man proceeded to sign a paper allowing Donald to go and take his state board exam. The man had already investigated and found out that Donald only had a few more hours to complete.

Although it was a very cold day in Chicago; cold enough that if you spit it would freeze into a pebble of ice as it hit the ground and rolled away seeking its own shelter, Selena and Donald were so grateful they ran down the street to a church they had seen. They kneeled down on its steps and thanked God. Donald kept his scheduled appointment to take his exam, and shortly after, received his cosmetology license. Selena says God always went in front and worked things out for her because she has always kept him first.

Donald left the shop a few times. The story of the first time he left comes to mind. Another beautician owned a shop not too far from Selena's; she felt that if she could influence Donald to work for her, she could really build her business. She offered him several empty promises and perks that never came to pass. Donald soon realized it was a mistake to leave Selena's, but his pride wouldn't allow him to admit it.

One day the shop was overflowing with customers and Selena was missing him; she had also heard that he wasn't too happy either. Selena grabbed some boxes, drove to the salon that Donald was working in and walked past everyone, straight to Donald. Everyone was shocked, but no one was more surprised than Donald. His mouth flew wide open as Selena approached him.

"Get your stuff, Donald!" she told him. Following orders, he packed his stuff. "Let's go," Selena said, after helping him add the last of his equipment to the boxes. Donald followed Selena out to her car with a huge grin on his face…he loved it! The other times he left would be decades later, and every time he returned.

Selena's grand opening was spectacular! Her entire family was there; her parents, her siblings, her husband, Elmer, and their three children. Her newfound friends, operators, clients and admirers were there in full force. It was like a wedding; in a sense it was. Her commitment to her business was like a marriage. In fact, she always said, she married her shop.

Elmer, slightly proud, yet uncomfortable with Selena's entrepreneurial spirit, was constantly argumentative, perhaps out of fear, insecurity, and jealousy. He himself, expressed a sense of regret when he confided in me, not long before he died as I was taking him for a ride in my new car. He pointed to a brick building and admitted that his head was once as hard as the bricks on that building. He confessed, if he had just listened to her, his life could have been so different; their lives together could have been different. Then he shook his head and ended with the statement that his ex-wife, my grandmother, Selena, was smart, something like Mrs. Roosevelt, and he was still proud of her.

He really didn't know any better. He was young and had no one to talk to him in a positive manner. He was never given any guidance on being a supportive husband, except for the times his brother, Perry, tried, which he never put any stock in. All he knew was that he should be the breadwinner, which he did very well, and that the wife should stay home and take care of the children.

It would be years later, before he realized what a blessing he had possessed in his wife, who wanted to work and grow together as a couple, a team, a unit, so to speak, to build a more comfortable life.

Selena would tell Elmer to come and sit in the shop and see how nice it was evolving. Elmer would come in, speak to everyone, and then sit in the reception area. He'd sit down with his newspaper held up to his eyes unless he wanted to see someone or something in particular. Such as the time Nat "King" Cole, came from the House of Nelson's after having his hair done to Selena's House of Beauty for a manicure. Elmer lowered the paper, just barely to the middle of his eyes, as if no one could see him watching. Then looking over the top of the paper, he knew his ears had not deceived him. It was Nat in the flesh, the man with the velvet voice, standing just a few feet away from him requesting a manicure.

Everyone was thrilled to be in his presence, especially Donald, who was enjoying a well-deserved break while his client was under the dryer. Donald sat in his chair with his legs crossed and his foot arched and pointed as usual. Donald asked Nat for his autograph. Nat looked around as if looking for paper or something. "Where should I write it?" he asked.

Donald lifted his leg and pointed to his ankle. "You can just sign right here, Mr. Cole," he said.

Mr. Cole signed it and proceeded to the manicure table; shaking hands and smiling at the shop full of fans before taking his seat. Donald didn't wash his ankle for a month.

Elmer's insecurity finally got the best of him. He began to seek refuge and comfort in the wrong places and arms. He began cheating again. Selena didn't dwell on the time that she and Elmer took the children over to one of Elmer's sister's for Sunday dinner and there was a lady in the window next door to his sister's house, waving and giving him signs. Elmer was trying to signal to the woman that his wife and children were with him. The lady either did not understand his signals, or she did not care because she kept grinning and waving until Elmer went over to the passenger side of the car to assist his wife and family as they were exiting the car.

Once she clearly saw his family, especially Selena, her grin faded, as if it were on an Etch A Sketch after being shaken up. Selena knew Elmer's sisters didn't care much for her because of the way she dressed with her clothes to fit her. They also didn't like her spirit of independence and the fact that they were not able to influence her way of thinking. However, they didn't dislike her enough not to live in her home until they could secure their own.

One sister burned Selena and Elmer's couch with a cigarette while living with them and when she was able to leave, she begged Selena to loan her one and only suitcase to her with a promise to send it back...she never did. Both of Elmer's sisters were constantly badgering him about his wife in some form or another.

However, that Sunday afternoon it became quite clear why Elmer had been spending so much time at this sister's house; she had been, as the old folks would say, "cloaking" for her brother and his side dish, the woman next door. Selena let him know that she was aware of it, and, of course, after his continuous denials, he shrank into a nut roll. This did not appease Selena. He stayed away from his sister's for a while.

Chapter Eighteen

Time had passed and this particular evening, Elmer came home and broke the news that he had gotten someone pregnant. It was a dreadful confession. Selena was hurt, but she remained strong. Selena was not so much stunned, as disappointed in his lack of discretion and responsibility. Selena knew he had a roving eye because of his past indiscretions.

This made Selena reflect back on memories of her parents' disputes when she was a child in Mississippi about her dad's affair with Ms. Gladys. Now, lo and behold, as a grown woman, she was experiencing the same betrayal in her own marriage. It showed that some things never changed. It has brought her to the realization that she still believes to this day…a man will go with a tree if it has a hole in it and you give him some Vaseline.

In the end, Selena felt that she and Elmer needed some time apart. As she immersed herself deeper into her work, Selena stayed on her mission. After apologizing, Elmer obliged and left. He went to New York to stay with one of his sisters. During his visit, he became so ill with grief, he had to be hospitalized for a while.

Meantime, Elmer wrote letters to Selena and their children, promising to send money when he could. He still expressed his love and concern, but Selena was working so hard and doing so good in her business that, although she may have liked for him to send some financial help for his children, she did not depend on it, nor was she looking for it.

I am certain after Selena had worked all day and all night, when she had a moment to herself in the wee small hours of the morning, thoughts of her husband and their marriage crept into her mind. Once she prayed, she weighed her options, though. She thought perhaps she could have dealt with the outside pregnancy, if this was his first act of infidelity, because he was still asking to come back home.

However, Selena continued to ponder and pray about the situation. Elmer gave her space and time, even when he returned to Chicago, but he always made it clear that he wanted to come back home to his wife and family. Nonetheless, Selena's thoughts and reflections led her in a different direction. Though the outside pregnancy could have been a hurdle that they could have over come together, the constant arguing, his habitual drinking, the severe lack of encouragement and support had been disturbing to her for quite some time anyway.

Those issues had compounded the situation to the point that she did not want him back…she didn't want that lifestyle of constant bickering back so she told him no. He was a bit heartbroken, but he accepted her decision. I say a bit heartbroken because I know he wasn't lonely for long; I'm sure the pregnant woman was waiting for him. How long would it last was the question because he still loved his wife. Let's face it. Anybody may want a vacation every now and then, but home is where the heart is.

Chapter Nineteen

After her separation, Selena's business was booming like the Fourth of July. It was always busy, so busy that her former boss, Ann, asked her if she wanted to take over the salon in the Pershing Hotel. Selena jumped at the offer after Ann assured her that she was serious. Selena's House of Beauty was now serving the community from two locations. They were two of the largest hotels at the time in Chicago, which allowed and catered to Negroes, especially celebrities.

Both beauty shops were fully staffed with top stylists and colorists offering press and curls, Lustrasilks, color from temporary to permanent, cuts, eyebrow arches; you name it they did it. The permanent relaxer, which stemmed from the conk and the process, complete with a roller set or finger waves, was becoming the new money maker.

There was never a dull moment at either salon. The hotels were in the same block right down the street from each other. One day you might see James Brown and Sarah Vaughn outside, sitting on top of Sarah's car, laughing and clowning. Sammy Davis, Jr.'s wife had just made headlines the day she came in the shop after purchasing so many pairs of shoes. Even Moms Mabley would play checkers with my young uncle El until time for her to head to the venue that she was scheduled to perform. Red Foxx would tell jokes while having a manicure sometimes.

The real colorful characters on the scene everyday were the pimps, prostitutes and boosters. Selena didn't condemn any of them. In fact, some of them became lifelong customers and friends of hers.

Finally Selena and Elmer divorced and the children lived with their mother. Selena was very busy with little time to reflect on anything but her children and businesses. As word spread about her recent divorce, men were flocking to her like bees to honey with offers of support. Though most were wishful thinking on their part because Selena the lady she was, was very selective. Selena was not ready for anything serious or time consuming. The wounds were still pretty fresh from her divorce. She was very protective over her heart, as well as over her children.

Selena loved and appreciated staying busy; she would walk back and forth between her two salons checking on things. Sometimes the clients themselves would walk back and forth between the salons…they didn't want to miss a moment of the happenings.

One day in particular, a gentleman was having his hair cut at the "House of Nelson's" and his chair happened to be facing the window as Selena took one of her daily walks between her salons. The gentleman was so impressed with both her signature walk and her smile that he got up from the chair, reached in his pocket. The business man that he was, he pulled out a thick roll of cash. He peeled off a $500 bill and handed it to one of the errand boys in the barber shop and requested that he take it to the lady with the pretty walk. The errand boy was so stunned he was just standing there with his mouth open. The gentleman then peeled off a twenty dollar bill and gave it to the errand boy for himself.

The boy ran breathlessly until he caught up with Selena in her Pershing salon. The errand boy handed the $500 bill to Selena. As he handed it to her, he told her, "The gentleman who gave me this $500 to give to you, told me to tell you he had never seen any woman walk that pretty before in his life. He said he would love to meet you, but if he could only see you walk again, he wouldn't be satisfied, but he would be happy."

Selena stunned and flattered screamed "What?" mainly, because she had never seen a $500.00 bill before in her life. The gentleman certainly had her attention and she did agree to meet him.

Greg was an intelligent, light-skinned, handsome gentleman with what they referred to back then as "good hair." Greg was a businessman with several legitimate businesses; like Selena's brother, Paul, Greg owned a barbeque house, but he also owned a sandwich shop and a dry cleaner.

Between their busy schedules, the two of them occasionally went to the movies and dinner together. Greg always helped her anyway he could, although Selena stressed that she did not want to engage in a serious relationship. She wasn't ready, being a recent divorcee. He understood and continued to offer his words of wisdom, as a business man, and his shoulder to lean on, as a friend. They remained good friends for life.

Selena had been holding onto the $500.00 bill that Greg had sent her for months and figured now was the perfect time and place to use it.

Selena finally found a new apartment that she liked. It was recommended through a friend of hers that was a barber at the House of Nelson's, next door to her Mansfield salon. Josephine and her husband lived in a nice building on 79th and Langley. When the apartment became available, "Little Jo," as she was affectionately called by Selena, due to her small petite frame and to separate her from any other Josephine, thought it would be nice for Selena and her three children. Jo and her husband would keep a watchful eye and ear out for Selena's children when they were home from work.

Selena and her three children moved into their new apartment, however they were not alone for long. Selena's mother Mary moved in with them shortly after. It worked out perfectly, both of Mary's younger daughters were then married and out on their own. Mary still worked as a domestic for the rich white people on the North side, but she was usually home before Selena.

Selena worked around the clock most of time, coming home so tired she would crawl into bed still wearing her uniform and shoes. She would be just that exhausted. I recall my Uncle El telling me how his mother, my grandmother, was often so tired, he would hear her crying herself to sleep from sheer exhaustion. The love, sympathy and appreciation he had for his mother prompted him to go in, remove her shoes, rub her feet and back. Before either of them realized it, Selena had fallen off to sleep after El managed to make her laugh.

In spite of the grueling schedule, things were looking good for Selena and her children through her hard work, with the help of her mother on the home front and good friends like Greg on the business side.

Wouldn't you know it, such as life would have it, a new challenge loomed on the horizon? Selena's children, now pre-teen and teen aged, began experiencing challenges as they traveled to and from school. Though the high school that her daughters attended for a short while was integrated with both Negro (black) and white students. The white students were prejudiced; however, it was the Negro students bullying and terrifying Selena's daughters and some of their friends.

The bullies envied how nice their clothes were and how nicely done their hair always looked. They were jealous of anybody they felt was better off than they were. One day the bullies actually broke the nose of one of Selena's daughters' friends on the way home from school.

Selena went up to the school the following day to express her concern about the safety of her own children and their friend who had her nose broken. Selena informed the school officials that she worked hard to be able to buy her children nice things and she was not going to sit back and allow them to be terrorized by these bullies any longer. The officials promised to look into the matter. That did not suit Selena. She then promised the officials that if the bullies break one of her daughters' noses or hurt them in any kind of way, there would be trouble. Either the bullies weren't warned properly, or they didn't care about the warning.

One day, not long after Selena's meeting with school officials, the bullies were back. They followed Selena's daughters and their friends to their homes, walking on the back of the frightened girls' shoes; torturing them with verbal abuse while shoving them.

They were like a gang of monsters on their trail. The gang of bullies was so bold, they tried to force their way into Selena's apartment, but Selena's mother, Mary, was there to greet them with a butcher knife in her hand and with words and names that were so sharp coming from her mouth they cut like razors. As Mary was facing the bullies, Selena was coming up the stairs behind the girls. Selena warned and threatened the girls and she was not empty handed, she had her thirty-eight pistol in her hand. Those bullies slowly and gently worked their way down the stairs past Selena and did a fifty yard dash out of the building.

There was peace, but only for a little while. The peace was slightly disturbed when a few boys robbed Selena's son, El, on his way to school; they took his lunch money. As the four boys surrounded El, one grabbed him by his collar, while the others searched his pockets. Selena was quite upset and shaken up as was the entire family, especially El, who experienced the encounter. After making sure El wasn't hurt, Selena and the family calmed themselves down as they thanked God.

Chapter Twenty

Selena's two shops were thriving so fast, it didn't matter if an operator chose to leave because there was always another stylist waiting to take their chair. They rarely left Selena's during those days because to leave Selena's would be to leave the in crowd.

Selena and her employees were working their hustle just as hard as everybody else; the pimps, the whores and the boosters were always on the scene. A motley crew, they put on as much of a show as the entertainers did right there on Cottage Grove.

Pole was a short, not so handsome, man, but his confidence was tough enough to keep a string of ladies, which were professional boosters. Kent had some of the prettiest girls on the track that ever lived. They were so naturally beautiful they could have been a part of Hollywood's elite screen legends. They were prettier than most of them including, Lena Horne, Dorothy Dandridge. Today Janet Jackson and Halle Barry were and are gorgeous but they had nothing on them. Kent stayed sharp in his tailor made suits while driving his blue Cadillac.

Slingshot was more extravagant; he cruised around in a hot pink Lincoln with his long lovely processed hair draped over the back of his headrest as he leaned back and watched the show from his ride. Slingshot always had an eye and an ear towards his money…he had some pretty girls, too.

Black Barry was blacker than ground coffee beans and as sharp as a straight edge razor. Black Barry's suits were tailor made out of silk. He was so together, from head to toe and beyond. Black Barry even had silk wallpaper on the walls in his apartment. Barry would drive up and down the Grove in his silver gray Cadillac just like the other pimps, watching and counting their money.

All of them would come inside of Selena's with their various stories and theories. Sometimes they were looking to recruit and enlarge their family while increasing their stock. Other times, they would be making sure their whores wouldn't be spending too much to maintain their beauty.

At one time, Black Barry had a girl sitting in every chair in the shop. He walked down the row of styling chairs, kissing each one of his girls on the hand. I remember hearing stories how each of them had looks of adoration and gratitude in their eyes. They seemed to feel so privileged to be one of his girls...part of his family. In some ways it's similar to gang members wanting and needing to feel like they belong to someone or something. It may not be the case with all prostitutes or gang members because some of them do come from loving, caring families and choose to rebel against their families. Most members of gangs and prostitution are weak minded followers who are easily manipulated by the con artist pimps, gang recruiters and gang leaders, whom they allow to take control of their minds. However, that's no reason to look down on them or hate them.

Only "for The Grace of God," it could be me or you. Of course, anyone who commits a crime should be punished and held accountable, but I don't think selling sex is a crime. It's morally wrong depending on one's own morals, but it is legal in some places.

The pimps didn't love money no more than Selena and her well-qualified staff of what was called hairdressers back then, who were always there and ready to service them and anyone else who wanted their hair done and had the money to pay for it. It was big pimping and big business on 64th and Cottage Grove. Regular working people, church-going people and partying people milled in and out of the shop. Sometimes there were all three types of people present at the same time.

People partied at the various hot spots. There was Club Delisa, then there was Bud Land and Robert's show lounge, just to name a few. No matter the category of people, they all flocked to Selena's to get their hair done first. Selena had top stylists working for her. Some worked for hair coloring manufacturers. Others worked for Ultra Sheen and other hair care companies.

They were masters in the art of hair, specializing in coloring, cutting, pressing, curling and eyebrow arching. As one completely satisfied client would exit Selena's, another one would be entering. Regular and new customers rotating, one after the other, searching for the same goal...to have their hair laid. This goal was achieved before they left Selena's. Selena's House of Beauty's reputation was quite the talk. Advertising is a great tool for a business, but positive word of mouth can be phenomenal.

New customers were always coming in, requesting a look they had seen on someone whom had had their hair done at Selena's. I recall hearing my grandmother speak about the time she had cut my aunt's hair who was a teen at the time. She finished it by lining it in the form of a "W" at the nape of her neck. A lady saw my aunt somewhere and wanted that same cut. She came to Selena's shop requesting to have her hair styled like this. However, the lady's texture of hair was quite different from my aunt's, which was, and still is, very fine and soft, making it easy to mold and lay down without heat or permanent relaxer, which the lady did not want. That lady did not understand why her natural hair would not lay like my aunt's hair, in spite of the fact that she absolutely wanted no parts of a press or relaxer.

There was never a dull moment at Selena's; clients came in weekly and biweekly. Ladies, working the track, greasing the spinning wheel, had to look good every day, all day. They would come in for service, every day or two. Some would come in twice a day, asking for a "retrace," after sweating their press and curl out; especially in the summer when it was too hot for a wig. A few might come back the same day requesting an entirely different look. A tint of a different color would make her less noticeable to a trick that she had just clipped. By the time the man woke up, when he did come looking for her, he wouldn't recognize her; her hair would be entirely different, including the color and, of course, she would change her outfit as well.

Selena was making more money by then; she started in the pantry of her kitchen, making 15 cents a head. Upon finishing beauty school, and becoming a licensed cosmetologist, she increased her rate to 50 cents a head. When she began working in Ann's salon, she was making $1.50 a head. Once she became the owner of her own salons, she increased her prices again making $2.00 to $3.00 a head and $5.00 for a Lustrasilk. She kept two wastebaskets by her booth; one for trash and the other for her money. At the end of the day, she would have a basket full of money, which she never ventured far from; she was in no way naive to the thought and actions of a thief.

This brings me to my next thought.

Stylists. You have to watch your equipment. One particular incident comes to mind. One of the stylists had pressed and curled this customer's hair so pretty, but   she stepped away from the client in her chair to check on her client under the dryer, allowing the client in her chair curls' to cool. When the stylist returned to style the lady's hair, she noticed her pressing comb was gone. It was nowhere to be seen, totally vanished.

The client sat there, waiting for the finishing touches of her style. Before the stylist combed the lady out she continued looking for her pressing iron. She proceeded to ask the other stylists did they borrow it or had they seen it. After receiving a unanimous no from all of them, she went back to her booth.

Selena stepped out of her office, away from her client and proceeded to help her operator look for the iron. After the other operators searched unsuccessfully, Selena asked the client had she seen the pressing comb.

The lady responded, "No."

Knowing that no one else had been in the booth, Selena very tactfully explained to the client that they didn't think she had stolen it, but perhaps it may have fallen into her purse by mistake. Selena then asked her to please check. With a look of bewildered hesitation, the lady opened her pocketbook and there it was, still warm wrapped in a towel. The entire shop gasped, but Selena, the peacemaker, held up her hand, still following the theme that the iron fell into her purse.

"See sometimes things happen like that. It must have fallen in there without you knowing it."

Everyone, following Selena's lead for peace, calmly allowed the lady to walk out of there after paying, of course, feeling as though her dignity was still intact. The lady was smart enough not to return for her prescheduled next appointment. After the pressing comb escapade, no one wanted to service her. That was a lesson learned by all. The customers learned "Don't try it," and the staff learned to watch, as well as work.

Chapter Twenty-One

❧

Selena found a new church on the south side. She had heard great things about it and began attending the various services as a visitor. She enjoyed the services there so much, it wasn't long before she joined. It was a huge congregation for those days; always packed full to capacity for morning and 11:00 p.m. broadcast service.

It was the First Church of Deliverance. Reverend Clarence H. Cobb was the founder and pastor, known as Preacher; he was so loved by so many. There were a few haters crossing the paths of him and his members. In fact, one day before Selena had the opportunity to get to know Preacher, a couple of ladies were talking with each other about their pastors, other people's pastors, the ones they liked and the ones they disliked, while sitting under the dryer.

It was customary that beauty culture schools taught students not to discuss politics or religion. I am not certain if they still stress that advice, but what does one do when the customers discuss those very touchy subjects, especially when parties involved are disagreeing? It's best to try to change the subject because this one lady under the dryer went on a warpath talking about "Preacher," saying how she could not stand him and nothing he stood for.

Little did she know, one of his faithful members was sitting across the shop in another chair, having her hair done.

She listened intently to her blatant disrespect and character assassination of Preacher.

By the lady being under the dryer, perhaps she didn't even realize how loud she was speaking. As busy as it was in the shop, quite a few, almost everyone, in fact, could hear her. Preacher's parishioner could not take it any longer. She excused herself from her stylist, walked to the loud mouth lady under the dryer, lifted the hood of the dryer and, in one swift motion, slapped her face. She practically begged her to say anything else bad about Preacher. "Now say something else about Preacher! I want you to. Try me."

The slap was so loud and hard the entire shop might as well had been in prayer because it was like silent night on that Saturday morning. The First Church of Deliverance member stood waiting for the lady to say another evil word against Preacher. No one in the shop spoke a word for at least a minute; waiting withheld breath to see if the lady under the dryer would speak or retaliate, which would escalate into a real fight....She did neither. The lady didn't speak or breathe. In fact, she never blinked her eyes. It remained quiet in the shop for a little while longer.

As a young child, I was told about that incident many times, but years later, when I became a licensed professional myself, and was still pretty young, I had the privilege of witnessing a similar situation.

It could have gotten real ugly and one of my coworkers was just as nervous as I was. A client, who considered herself to be a Christian, was ranting in a disrespectful way, concerning her opinion of Minister Farrakhan, while one of his devout members was present. My coworker and I knew how devoted to the Minister and the organization this lady was. We could see her eyes getting colder and slanting more with every negative slur the other woman spoke.

In fact, we witnessed her face go through many changes in a matter of seconds, resulting in an icy calm sort of like a melting icicle. While we were trying get one of them out of there quickly, the Muslim woman could tell we were nervous. She assured us she wouldn't hurt the sister. "I understand the sister is just lost," she said.

Meanwhile, Selena was becoming increasingly popular, running her two top-notch salons inside of two of the top hotels that catered to Negroes in Chicago. Selena had her own dressmaker, Mabel Page. It was a divine match. There is no better feeling than teaming up with a person who loves to perform a service that you need and you love the way they do it. Mabel loved designing and sewing, especially for Selena. They made each other look good. Once Mabel acquired Selena's measurements and made her a couple of outfits, Selena rarely had to come in for fittings.

Ms. Page had a keen eye and a scientific approach to tailoring Selena's garments with not a thread out of place. Ms. Page did the same for all of her clients. I remember Selena sharing the story of one of the many times she was wearing one of Mabel's signature designs. The dress was fabulous and Selena looked so beautiful in the dress. I mean she wore it well, so well that a very well-known singer saw her in it and offered to buy it off of her right then. The lady was well known for her style of singing. One of her songs was about a difference and a day. However, Selena would not sell her the dress, but she did give her Ms. Page's number.

It took a while and a few detours, but Selena was finally realizing two of her childhood dreams—that of making women look good by doing their hair, and having her clothes tailor made. She looked good, just like her mother did when Selena was a child.

Preacher, a well-dressed minister and businessman, loved the way Selena dressed and often invited her as part of his elite entourage to travel with him when he spoke in different cities. Preacher wasn't your ordinary minister; he was a power broker, a leader, a friend, as well as a father figure to many, he gave back. If someone didn't have food, rent, a place to live, he provided those amenities and necessities for them. Preacher built lifelong dedicated relationships while building his ministry. He was well respected, not only in Chicago, but all over the world.

When he went to another city and state, he didn't just make an appearance. He showed up, showed off and showed out. Not only were other ministers impressed with his leadership, but city council members were as well. He would often have invited meetings set up with mayors and other various politicians and ministers of the cities he visited. His spiritual guidance afforded people hope, in knowing that Jesus Is the Light of the World.

Reverend Cobb's ministry was the blueprint for many who followed him and those who stepped out on their own. First Church was a college course for many who wanted to know "This Is How It's Done," especially when it came to the First Church Choir. First Church's Choir was known all over the world, just as the pastor was. It wasn't just a given; they earned their respect. No choir could touch their anthems. They may have come close, but they couldn't reach them. That's like playing the lottery, having two out of three numbers …you lost. They could sing anything.

Choir directors, ministers of music and many musicians would flock to the 11:00 p.m. broadcast to watch, to listen and to concentrate; to get their lesson to take back to their prospective churches and choir rehearsals.

First Church had a team of well-trained musicians and first class directors to handle its huge massive choir.

Selena maintains to this day, ever since she joined First Church, she has never looked back, especially after doing Nana's hair. Yes, Preacher sent his mother and a few others to Selena to have their hair done. Now that was an endorsement and it spread like the wind.

Chapter Twenty-Two

Selena was living it up, managing her businesses, going out meeting new people and networking. Every time she stepped out of her shop, looking like success, with her hair always coiffed, a new client would follow her back in, hoping to come close to looking as good as she did.

With her mom at home in the afternoons and evenings with the children, Selena felt comfortable going out on the few evenings she was able to do so. Whether she was alone, or on a date, Selena's drink of choice was always the same, orange juice or 7-up. Always a lady, it was an extreme rare occasion that Selena used foul language.

The year 1956 proved to be an extraordinary year, but not without blemish; she was opening two salons, going through a divorce, becoming a single parent, moving to a new apartment, registering her children in new schools, while meeting a lot of new people and broadening her horizons. Selena's life was going through a new season.

Though success attracts admirers, it, just like a garden, has to be maintained to keep the weeds out. Living the life of success allows weeds in the form of haters to sometimes pop up. A lady, who happened to be renting a store front for her salon, next door to one of the hotels where Selena housed one of her salons, went downtown and filed a complaint with the city to have Selena's neighboring salon shut down. It did not work. The woman's efforts failed; the city replied that Selena had not broken any laws, therefore, nothing could be done about it.

As if that wasn't enough, the police informed Selena of an anonymous tip they received about her. The tipster had told the police that Selena was dealing drugs because her shops were much too busy. The police told her that they had to address it and they would have to search her residence after searching the shop. After finding nothing at her business they went to her apartment to perform a search. Her mother, Mary was there with her.

"WATCH 'EM! WATCH 'EM!" Mary shouted to Selena as the two of them followed the different officers through the apartment while they conducted the search. Mary was afraid that they might try to plant something. After finding nothing, the officers seemed pretty remorseful as they apologized for any inconvenience. Moreover, they told Selena that they would keep an eye on her as a precaution for her safety because somebody was really jealous of her and the success of her business. Noticing the despair in Selena's face, they repeated that they were just doing their job as they shared one other tidbit before leaving.

"During our investigation, we were told when you go to a lounge, you don't drink anything but orange juice."

It wasn't long after those weeds had been laid to rest, another one popped up. Thieves broke into Selena's apartment while no one was there and stole the money she had been saving to pay her income tax. Selena was upset, to say the least. Just the idea of her home being violated sickened her stomach. The thought of the many times she had clicked her curling irons to save her well-earned money put her in full defense mode. She began to watch everyone more carefully and, thereafter, opened a bank account with a safety deposit box. Selena made weekly deposits and began to relax a little. The fact that she never left home without her snub nose 38 added to her sense of security. While at work, the sadness in her heart was detected through her conversation.

One evening, "Sling Shot", the pimp, came in the shop and noticed Selena's smile was not as bright as usual. He asked her what the problem was and offered her his help. After all, money was no problem to Sling Shot. Selena exclaimed how someone had broken into her apartment and stole the money she had put away for her taxes.

"Money! I got that. How much you need, baby?" Sling Shot asked as he pulled out a couple of wads of money. Wads so thick and round they looked like toilet paper. It wasn't toilet paper, it was green back, cash and not just single dollar bills. Sling Shot was like a currency exchange, he had every denomination of a bill made that you could think of. Selena studied the rolls of money in Sling Shot's hands for a moment before looking him eye to eye while warning him...

"If you give me some money I am not going to give you none back."

He groaned ...

"I ain't looking for none back! Do you want this money or not, woman?"

Recognizing one of the main games of a pimp, Selena reiterated, "Okay, now, just 'cause you give me this, I am not going to give you any." Sling Shot told her to take the money. Selena took it, then they laughed and talked for a while, watching clients come and go. The end result was Selena was able to pay her taxes on time.

Soon after, she began looking for a new apartment. Selena finally found one she liked and put a deposit on it. When the time came for her to pick up the keys to the apartment, the woman in the rental office informed her that the apartment had been rented to someone else.

Disappointed and shocked, Selena stated that could not be true because they were holding her money for that apartment. The woman said it was true and they had nothing else available at this time.

Selena stood there in disbelief, as she watched the woman turn her back, walk back to her desk and take her seat, as though she had dismissed her. Selena walked briskly through the swinging double doors and asked the lady for her deposit. The lady responded that there was no money there in the office and that she would have to wait two or three weeks to receive her refund.

Selena turned to leave, but quickly turned around after processing how unfair the woman's statements sounded. Nothing added up in Selena's favor, but she knew this was not how to do business. She was not the one who changed or backed out of the agreement. There was a rolling table that separated Selena from the lady. Selena snapped, "GIVE ME MY MONEY!" as she hit that table so hard it rolled all over that office. Selena said the lady probably thought she had hit her, but by the time that table had stopped rolling the lady had placed Selena's money in her hand.

About a month later, Sling Shot came in the shop, ranting that he was low on cash and needed some help to make his ends meet. Selena walked right past him with her usual signature smile.

Sling Shot caught her attention when he specifically asked her if she could help him out, let him hold something.

Selena faced him, making sure they had eye contact as she did the prior month and told him she did not have any money. Before he could speak another word, Selena reminded him with calm certainty in her voice that she told him upfront that she was not going to give him any money.

Sling Shot smiled to himself, knowing he was testing the waters of her mind. She passed the test to him, any other pimps, wanna be pimps and regular everyday men.

The news quickly spread that Selena could have been a pimp, herself. She was diligent and of a very strong, sound mind. Most importantly, she was hard working, unlike most pimps who hardly work. Her mama and daddy taught her to be a lady, but not a fool. A man trying to seduce her and gain her confidence with his thoughts of the way things should go didn't fly with her. Selena had her own mind. She has always said give each person credit for their head.

Not to say she wouldn't help her man. Truth be known, for years she had worked together with her ex-husband to make ends meet, but he brought his paycheck home for her to cash and manage as she saw fit for the best benefit of their household.

Sling Shot was a pimp and his job, like every other pimp, was to manipulate the mind of a weak woman. This could only happen if she was weak minded. A pimp gained a woman's confidence and took complete control while she did all of the work and incurred all of the risk. The hardest thing a pimp had to do was count the money the woman has brought in through her labor, watch her and if she gets busted, bail her out with the money she had turned over to him in the first place. Believe me. If she was not making a good profit, he would leave her in there.

Growing up in the midst of her parents' roadhouse days helped Selena become aware of all kind of people and a lot of different circumstances. A conversation she heard as a child between her father Henry and one of her aunts, her mother's sister, was engraved in her memory for life.

Selena recalled how Daddy was sitting on the porch, watching the children play, and her aunt, her mother's sister, had just been dropped off by a man.

"Mr. Henry, can you let me have a cigarette?" (but, Auntie pronounced it cigaritt.)

Henry was fed up with his sister-in law's leaching; not only cigarettes, but food, shelter, everything. At the same time, she never felt like working. He looked up at her after pulling a drag off of his cigarette.

"Didn't you just get out of a car wit' a nigga? And you asking me for a cigarette? I bet your behind still wet... been out wit' a nigga all night , ain't even got a cigarette!"

At the time, Selena was too young to know what it meant, but the tone of Henry's voice let her know that it was something that she should pay attention to. She made note of it and as she grew into a young lady, she came into her own understanding as to what it meant.

Most everybody is born a fool. It's up to us as individuals whether we choose to live as a fool.

Selena's mother, Mary, always said, "You may be born a fool, but you don't have to stay a fool."

In other words, born a fool, live a fool, die a fool. Though she had no control over the first, Selena was determined not to do the latter two.

As hard as Selena worked, as a single parent of three, her motto was only a damn monkey would give her hard-earned money to a man that you know had a string of women whoring. She wasn't a whore and she was not interested in being a link in his chain. If anything, he would have had to become a link in hers.

Actually, Selena had no desire to be with any pimp. They could laugh and talk, but that was the extent of it, except when the pimp's girls or the pimp, himself, would have services done in the salon. After hours, the pimp's girls or the pimp would sit, talk and laugh with Selena, even asking her opinion on some things.

In fact, the pimps were usually complete gentlemen in her presence. They even tipped their hats to her, and when they weren't wearing one, they would tip their heads. All of the pimps and Selena had mutual respect for one another. They were all just making moves, trying to stay on the winning side of the game of life.

One day Black Barry approached Selena from a different angle. He wanted to do a joint venture with her, somewhere, on the outskirts of town. He felt that the two of them together could make a lot more money. Black Barry didn't want to go into details in the salon; too many eyes and ears, so he invited Selena to dinner one Sunday afternoon. Selena accepted the invitation and agreed to come after church.

Chapter Twenty-Three

Selena arrived that Sunday afternoon just in time for dinner. Black Barry's mother was an excellent cook and she helped her son manage their home, as well as the girls.

Black Barry's mother was putting the finishing touches on the table, while instructing the girls where each dish should be placed on the table. Black Barry had escorted Selena to a seat in the living room. He acknowledged that he was glad that she made it. Selena responded that she was interested in hearing what Black Barry had to say about this potential business for them because she was interested in making money, as long as it was legal, which he had insured her it was before convincing her to agree to the meeting.

Black Barry offered Selena a drink. Afterwards, he poured her request of a glass of orange juice. Selena looked around the apartment with admiration. She told him how beautiful his place was. He offered to give her a tour. It was a beautiful large apartment on the Southside of Chicago on 51st street.

The apartment had four bedrooms, which were elegantly decorated with lace and silk wallpaper. It had two full bath rooms; one which was connected to the master bedroom.

There was an enclosed back porch in the back and a sun parlor in the front, just off from the living room. French doors divided the two rooms. The living room, the dining room and the hallway had red silk wallpaper; the kitchen, the bathrooms and the bedrooms had white silk wall paper with black lace border.

Just as Selena and Black Barry completed the tour of his large 4 bedroom apartment, his mother called everyone to be seated in the dining room for dinner. Everyone took their seats around the elaborate dinner table.

"Everything smells so good and it looks good," Selena remarked as she flashed her signature smile to everyone, especially to the cook, Black Barry's mother. Barry's mother smiled back with a nod of pride and gratitude. Everyone bowed their heads for a moment of prayer as Black Barry blessed the table and food. Barry's mother had cooked so much food, the table was full of choices; many of Selena's favorites.

The meal consisted of baked chicken and dressing, candy sweet potatoes, smothered cabbage, hot buttered homemade rolls, cornbread and pot roast with carrots and potatoes. Bowls and platters were being passed until everyone was served. Selena had tasted the dressing, candy sweet potatoes and cabbage that was on her plate and loved all of it.

Just as she began to slice into her piece of baked chicken, one of the ladies of the house said something that evidently was disliked by Black Barry. Selena could not recall what the young lady had said to cause his enraged disapproval, but what she did remember and never forgot, was how angry Black Barry had become in an instant. Before anyone else could react to whatever the woman had said, Barry had slapped her so hard—he backhanded with such an enormous force that her chair flipped backwards, causing her legs to land on top of the dinner table. A couple of the other women helped their roommate up as she was covering her mouth, avoiding eye contact with everyone in the room, perhaps out of embarrassment.

Everyone else slowly returned to eating, everyone, that is, except Selena. She had laid her fork in her plate and sat back in her chair. Selena had completely lost her appetite; her stomach had turned...she was totally turned off as a woman and as a potential business partner... from the food that was set before her, to the blatant disrespect displayed toward a defenseless woman.

As a guest in his home, Selena was deeply disappointed by the disrespect Barry displayed in front of her. A man hitting a woman was, and is, a known no-no in Selena's mind. Any person hitting another is a no-no to her, but a man whose strength surpasses a woman's strength is unacceptable. Realizing that the mere mention of words, no curse words, just words expressing the woman's thoughts angered him to that degree was unbelievable to Selena. In her mind, Black Barry's actions were that of a coward.

Barry had finished everything on his plate; when he looked over and saw Selena just sitting there with almost as much food on her plate as when they began eating, he figured that she wanted to get straight to the business at hand. Barry rose from the table and asked Selena to join him in the living room. Selena glanced around the room at everyone eating, as if nothing had happened. Even Barry's mother was eating, as if the interruption had never occurred.

Selena got up from the table and followed him toward the front. The two of them took a seat in the living room. Black Barry began to apologize to Selena for having to witness the encounter; I guess he felt the vibe of dislike and disappointment from Selena. Before he completed his statement, Selena interrupted him by holding her hand up and telling him whatever business venture he thought that they could do together would be impossible.

Barry interrupted with protests. "Why? Wait! Let me explain!"

Selena didn't wait for the explanation of his actions. She repeated that there was no way that the two of them—him and her, could ever do anything together because if he were to hit her like he had hit that girl, (while pointing toward the dining room), she wouldn't tolerate it.

"You would never be able to go to sleep, because I would kill you while you sleep if you hit me!"

Barry persisted with trying to get Selena to relent and change her mind. Finally, realizing that he could not change Selena's mind about the incident, him, or the business venture, Barry relinquished the idea and accepted that his venture wasn't going to happen the way he planned it.

Selena grabbed her purse as she stood to leave; Black Barry escorted her to the door. Thereafter, they remained cordial toward one another and maintained mutual respect as they continued to run their own separate businesses.

However, Barry never gave up on his idea. Eventually, he decided to do it on his own. The initial plan was Black Barry wanted him and Selena to buy a place on the outskirts of town; just off the highway where they would house the girls and entertain the gentlemen. Barry's idea was before Hugh Hefner and his playboy mansion and way before the Bunny Ranch. He wanted Selena to help him run the place and send some of her operators out to the place to keep the ladies looking good.

Barry dreamed of how big their business could be, of how beautiful their names would look bright and bold on a place just off of the highway, along with the combination of their good taste, he knew the place could and would have been magnificent.

Black Barry already had clients out that for the girls. They seemed to always enjoy the young ladies and were willing to spend money. It was a weekend thing.

Either he would send or take a couple of the ladies out there on Fridays, and they would return on Sundays with plenty of money. This gave Barry the idea that if the ladies were accessible on a daily basis, there would be no end to how much money he could make.

Barry, through the help of one of his regular customers, found an old farm house available for rent with option to buy in a rural area that he thought was perfect. He hired a few handy men, from Chicago that he knew and a few from out there in the boondocks, to fix the place up. It didn't cost him a lot of money. It was a give and take, sort of a barter situation.

So many hours of work granted each man time with one of the women. Barry bought new furniture for the house each of the bedrooms had new bedroom sets. It was laid out and the men were flocking to the place; before work, after work, lunch time or dinner time, whatever worked best for the "john".

Barry still had a string of women working the streets of Chicago and maintained his immaculate South Side apartment while building his extended business.

As usual, Blacks, Negroes and coloreds have had great money making ideas, regardless whether they match everyone's ethical standards or not. They still turn out to be profitable money making ideas.

However, when and if, they turn out to be extremely profitable, especially back in those days, it could cause a problem. Not only does success breed hate, jealousy and dissention, even from your own people, it can be worse when white folks think you're making too much money that's double trouble.

Colored or Negro, which is what we were called back then, now Blacks, have produced a lot of great inventions. Unfortunately, if the government, which was ran by white folks, (some, not all, but most) could not figure out a way to profit from the black person's idea, they would annihilate and amputate the idea to the point that there was nothing left of the person who thought of it.

They not only killed the dream, they assassinated the spirit of the dreamer. This is what was about to happen to Black Barry and his dream; just as it happened to the game of policy. Think about it. As long as the Negroes ran the numbers, it was illegal. The "white folks" took it, made it legal and called it the lottery; as they did in many other circumstances. Sadly enough, we, as Blacks, do it to ourselves and each other these days, by tearing each other down and not supporting one another.

Some of the more well-to-do white men got word and some of them enjoyed the services of Barry's business first-hand. In between the happy hours of being serviced by some of the most beautiful women, the men began tabulating and guesstimating how much money Barry's operation was bringing in.

Usually when one is doing well enough to capture the attention of the so-called "shot callers," they want in; they want a cut. Sometimes a cut is not satisfactory, though. Sometimes they want it all; meaning they threaten one's life, or have them shut down completely, based on fabricated codes and legalities.

In this case, they threatened Barry with shutting him down, but he felt that he had enough clients who would support him. That held them off for a while. Barry had been operating the new location, just shy of a year, when the authorities raided the farmhouse and locked everyone up.

Barry, who was in Chicago, at the time, received a message that the authorities were looking for him. It wasn't clear whether he turned himself in, or just left town. Before leaving, Barry gave money to a couple of the ladies to try to bail the other ladies out of jail and hired a gentleman to drive them. Another thing he did was called Selena and offered her his apartment, which he knew she loved, after explaining that he had to go away.

Selena did love the place, and she had been looking for a new place, so she accepted his offer with no strings attached. Barry even worked it out with the landlord who was fine with transferring the rent responsibility to Selena.

Selena was happy about the four-bedroom apartment, complete with the silk wallpaper and two bathrooms. There was a bedroom for Selena, her mother, her son and one for her two daughters to share. In order to make her ends meet and subsidize her being a single parent, she would rent out her son's bedroom and he would sleep on a sofa bed in the dining room.

Some rooms had white silk wall paper and others had red. Selena purchased white leather furniture for the living room and black and white tweed carpet. I was always told how sharp the apartment was. The only con to living there was though Selena had given her children specific instructions that they were not to open the door for anyone, not even to her, (which she was exaggerating), if she and their grandmother weren't home because of it being a well-known adult entertainment house, often referred to as a "whore house".

Due to the nature of business that Barry ran and his sudden vacation the clients were not aware that there were new tenants in the apartment. As often as they kept coming by, it was as if they did not care who lived there, they wanted the same service, which they had become accustomed to.

The milkman might be knocking on the front door, the garbage man would be at the back door, and the postman might be pecking on one of the windows. It didn't matter some man was always trying to get in, until they finally got the message.

When Selena or her mother Mary, were home they would holler through the doors and the windows that those people no longer lived there. Eventually, the johns stopped coming by.

Chapter Twenty-Four

❦

Shortly thereafter, Selena bought a new car; a brand new black and white hard top convertible Ford. It was sharp, the top was hard, but it reverted into a space between the trunk and the back seat. It was hot! Brand new off the showroom floor!

It was so sharp when Selena drove up in front of her shop clients, employees, everybody ran out to see it. They loved watching the top go up and down with the push of a button. (This was in the mid-1950s).

The last time Selena let the top down, as many as the car would hold jumped in for a ride; some customers were still wearing the comb out capes and clips in their hair. Some of the stylists were still holding either a comb or a brush. Even the rain that began to fall didn't put a damper on that day. Once she dropped off one group, another was waiting to get in and ride. They rode in the rain with the top down for a quite a while.

That was Selena's first brand new car; no one else had driven it. It not only looked good, and smelled good, it rode good. It was a blessing. She was able to get to and from work in no time, especially when she took the route through Washington Park. A few blocks down Cottage, turn left into Park and she was home in a matter of minutes, which was well appreciated, when she needed to get home quickly to check on her children.

There were times when Mary would still be at work and was in the beginning stages of opening her own soul food restaurant.

Selena's daughters were teenagers now, and the boys were hanging around. One boy, whom Selena did not approve of, liked her fourteen-year-old middle daughter, Juanita. Selena told the boy that Juanita was not allowed to receive company when she wasn't home.

Once Selena found out the boy was often in trouble, this prompted her to revoke his welcome completely. Selena then told him to stay away from her daughter and her home, period. The boy ignored Selena's rules and request. Consequently, Selena found out where he lived and went to speak with his mom. She pleaded with his mother to keep him away from her daughter and their home. Selena's feelings regarding the boy's uncontrolled disrespect were confirmed when his mother whined that she couldn't do anything with him. Selena left but not before, confirming the lady's stand on the situation, which was that she couldn't do anything or control anything concerning her son.

Selena quickly regrouped and said, "Okay," as she turned and left the woman's home.

A few days later, the boy and a friend of his returned to Selena's home while she was at work and her three children were home alone. Although Selena had instructed the boy to stay away and her children not to let him in, the boy insisted on ringing the bell constantly, feverishly beating on the door in the vestibule and shouting for them to let him in.

There was a telephone in the apartment, but due to Selena's children abusing its use by constantly talking on it, causing the line to stay busy all of the time, Selena put a lock on the phone. They could only receive calls, not make them. Though Juanita had figured out how to make calls, in spite of the lock, the boy's persistence obviously terrified her so that it did not even occur to her.

After being told several times by each one of Selena's three children, the boy still refused to take no for an answer. This prompted Selena's son, El, to sneak out of the back, down the stairs and to a pay phone to call his mother. El explained to Selena how he and his two sisters begged the boy to leave and told him that they could not let him in, but he would not leave. In fact, he was still there.

Juanita was still asking him, "Please go away. Stop shouting and banging on the door. Please leave!"

El ran back home, crept his way back into the apartment, without the boy or his friend knowing that he had ever left. It was only a few minutes before Selena arrived home. She parked down the block, in order for the boy and his friend not to notice that she was coming.

Selena pulled the then removable seatbelt and buckle from her new car, wrapped it around one of her hands, while holding her 38 pistol in the other hand. When she made it into the entrance of the building, the boy and his friend were still laughing and clowning so much with their backs to the street that they had not noticed that Selena had crept in on them. When the two of them turned and saw Selena, their eyes grew as large as silver dollars, but you could have bought them for a penny. They were paralyzed with shock.

However, Selena didn't give them any time to catch their breath. When the friend saw the gun in her hand, he took off running as fast as he could. Selena was beating the want to-be invader with the seatbelt and buckle, while promising to shoot him if he raised his hand. With every lick, she verbally reminded him of the many times that she had asked, pleaded, and warned him not to come back. The first break Selena took from beating him, he promised her that he would not come back. Finally, Selena stepped aside and allowed him to pass her, still holding the pistol and seatbelt as he exited. Knowing Selena didn't play, he never returned and he never retaliated.

On to the next venture, Selena was hard at work again when a woman came in for Selena to service her hair. The lady was finally seated in Selena's chair. Selena began examining the lady's hair and scalp and noticed that the woman's scalp was covered with green puss-filled sores and scabies. Selena stopped and quickly washed her hands.

After washing and drying them thoroughly, she went in the back of the salon and mixed up a potent scalp ointment for the woman. Selena gave the mixture to the woman with instructions to use it daily for two weeks. The woman used Selena's concoction and returned to the salon two weeks later. Everyone, including the staff, the woman herself, as well as Selena, were surprisingly thrilled by the results; her scalp was completely healed clear of all of the sores.

This ignited a new spirit in Selena's entrepreneurial mind. Selena went on a mission to find out how to mass market her scalp cream. She found the place to purchase the jars for her scalp cream, but Selena became torn between her scalp cream and the idea that a new friendly acquaintance had proposed to her. The friend constantly called Selena, trying to convince Selena to come and take this class that she and her sister were beginning to teach. The friend's sister had been working in a wig shop, assisting women with their wig and wiglet purchases.

All of that fitting, styling and pinning on hair with hairpins and rubber bands gave this pretty lady, who happened to be the hired help, a brilliant idea. Though Christine Jenkins had beautiful hair of her own, she began to realize the effect and the importance of hair, or the lack of it, to people in general, especially women. Christine had a light bulb moment one day while in her kitchen. Noticing the rack, which she had placed her dish towel on, she began to visualize it in a different way. There were three long arms which extended from the hinges on the wall in a swinging formation.

Thus, the idea for the first "Hair Weev" machine, which was a patented spelling for the authentic technique that was developed by Mrs. Jenkins for adding commercial hair to one's own hair through the art of Hair Weev Technology, using a three cord method, was born.

Christine had created and mastered the steps to the technique and shared them with her sister, Rose, who was a hairstylist. Rose told Selena about this technique that would allow her to make more money for her time.

Rose exclaimed to Selena how her sister, Christine, had invented this technique for adding hair and had already taught her first class and was preparing to teach her second class soon, due to her plans to move from Chicago with her husband. Rose told Selena that she knew that she would be good at it, as successful as her two salons already were. Selena promised Rose that she would think about attending the class.

Rose informed Selena about the price of the class, where it was to be held and the scheduled date. Selena filed it in the back of her mind and continued to concentrate on her scalp cream. Selena had saved enough money to purchase the jars for her scalp cream and had made plans to pick them up.

It was getting closer to the date of the "Hair Weev" class. Rose was continuously calling Selena to remind her of the urgency for her to take this class, especially now due to her sister leaving for Cleveland soon. She took time to convince Selena how good this new thing would be for her, as well as her business. Still, Selena's reply was the same as before. "I'm going to try to make it. I am still thinking about it."

The day came when Selena was heading south on Cottage Grove on her way to purchase the jars when something jolted her (probably The Spirit of The Living God), and in a split second, just before approaching a viaduct, Selena made a U turn, changed her mind, and decided to use that money to take the class.

Selena figured she could get the jars later, but, that she had better seize the opportunity of this innovation while it was being offered. First of all, Selena has always loved, and still loves being first. Though it was Christine Jenkins' second class, it was the first one Selena had been invited to participate in. The first class was taken by a very few students. Some were relatives who were also stylists.

Ms. Jenkins was preparing to move to Ohio, and Rose was preparing to move to California; in their quest to share this new horizon, they were able to reach out and convince a few other Chicago hairstylists to take the class before the two of them left. There were a few other stylists with pretty good salons with a good clientele base and they made a decent income with Christine Jenkins' method of authentic "Hair Weeving" and the small group of them became a close knit clique.

However, in all of their success, none of them achieved the

great feat that Selena would soon accomplish. This new service would become a game changer for Selena.

❧

Selena arrived, ready to take the class. Ms. Jenkins and Rose showed her the technique once, and as I have heard her say all of my life, in five minutes she had it! Selena says she watched them one time and asked them to move away from her while she tried it on her own. Moments later, after rotating from one student to another, they saw that Selena had it!

After a few days of meeting and making new friends, Selena returned to work and began to practice and perfect her new craft.

Selena began advertising her new craft by having the "Hair Weev" logo added to the windows of her salons. Some clients and operators were inquisitive, while others rebuked this new trend. A couple of the operators wanted nothing to do with the added hair clientele.

One of her stylists stated he didn't want to style anyone with all of that hair on.

Upon hearing about the new method, one of her operators, Mr. Woodhouse, said, "I don't want any of those," as he pointed to a hair weev client.

Selena gave him her bright signature smile and said, "Okay." Selena was a mover, a real go getter. She did not like arguing. It was a waste of time and energy. She was an executive with no time for excuses or rebellion. If one won't, another one will, was her motto. If that way don't work, there is always another way.

Her objective...get it done and done was whatever it was. "Can't" and "no" were not a part of Selena's vocabulary. There were plenty of other operators in both salons willing to make that money and money they made, honey, especially her first right hand/manager Sammy.

Whatever she needed Sammy to do, whether it was styling hair, collecting money, or teaching a new operator how to work on weeved hair, he did, until he passed away after he had become ill. It was hard and painful to lose such a good and trusting friend, but Selena's faith and resilience helped her to bounce back. Although she had hoped and prayed that Sammy would get well, she had a little warning time, due to his illness. Unlike the time when another dear friend and talented co-worker/employee named Spinx died.

Spinx had received a letter from the IRS (Internal Revenue Service) one day, and it worried him so much, he went home and died. He never woke up the next morning. No warning at all. He was just gone the next day.

"Spinx could do some hair!" is the story I always heard everyone say when referring to Spinx, especially Selena. Selena distinctly remembered at his funeral, just staring at his hands, thinking. "Look at those hands. They could do some hair!"

The customers who wore "weevs" hairstyles cost more to style than a regular style because the stylist had to deal with more hair, added hair. The breeze of all that money walking past Mr. Woodhouse's chair was leaving him and his pockets a little chilly. One day, with a smile on his face, he said to Selena, "I'll take one of those."

"Oh, okay," Selena responded. It was like an assembly line.

Selena being the only one in her salon to have taken the "Hair Weev" class, therefore, she was the only one there able to service the "hair weev" clients. Her profits began to increase so much and the demand was growing so fast that she began looking for a new store large enough to house both of her staffs from her two salons, and one with enough room for her to have a private office.

The technique was taught to be done in a private setting, not out in the open. It was a great idea and greatly appreciated for the person who had spent their hard earned money to take the course, and an even better idea for the potential client. It left them, and still leaves them, with a sense of dignity and privacy, which helped to enhance the comfort ability of wearing an authentic hair weev.

Selena's became like an elite club of people, women and men looking to achieve satisfaction in the ultimate beauty experience. Just like any other good thing in life, it depends on the person. Some people see, learn, or experience something so good, they want to share it with others, even if it's only a few. On the other hand, some people find a good thing and it becomes their best kept secret, and they want to keep it to themselves.

Selena was making so much money that she gave up doing regular hair all together. No more shampoo, presses and curls for her. Her well-trained staff had watched her blend and coif the commercial hair with a person's natural hair long enough to masterfully and meticulously execute great results on every head.

Things were shifting in a great, positive and prosperous way for Selena. Selena credits herself for always being a go getter, not a quitter, but she shall never forget the spirit and teachings of her pastor, as was written earlier, "Preacher," Reverend Clarence H. Cobb and her church, "The First Church of Deliverance." Jesus Is The Light of the World! Ever since she joined there, she says she never had to look back, especially after preacher had enough respect and faith that he sent his own mother for Selena to do her hair.

However, when Selena stopped doing regular hair, quite a few of her clients didn't want to wear a weev, but for every one who didn't, there were three or more new clients that did. Some of Selena's clients would beg her to please just shampoo their head, even if she couldn't complete them. They loved the way she shampooed.

Selena says no matter what else you're having done to your head, a shampoo is one of the most important parts of your hair do. In fact, it's the basis of it.

Chapter Twenty-Five

❦

I remember at age seventeen, soon to turn eighteen, being a student at Pivot Point Beauty School. At the time my mother was allowing me to shampoo her head and checking out my skills at one of my grandmother's salons.

After I completed my mother's shampoo, my grandmother, Selena, inspected my mother's hair and made me do it over right away. It was not clean, she said, and she was not going to have me, one of her descendants, her eldest grandchild in beauty school, surrounded by professionals, not knowing how to shampoo properly. To this day, she praises me for shampooing like her, an expert, not missing a spot. I learned to work like my grandmother, unlike those who pat and tap in a hurry to get finished with tunnel vision concerned only with the money for today, not interested in building a return clientele base with money flowing, instead of trickling.

Selena made plans to take the Advanced Class and the Teacher's training from Ms. Jenkins. The classes were held in Cleveland, Ohio. When Selena arrived, she taught the teachers something; they were highly impressed with Selena's enhancement to the technique and asked her to share with the entire class.

Hair Weeving and Selena together were like Genesis, which kept unfolding revelations. Her new beginning kept evolving, getting better and brighter. Selena learned every facet of the technique that Christine and Rose had taught her; she learned how to consult with the customer, hand/hair loom or hand weft the hair because back then hair was not machine wefted and readily available for use often. Selena learned where, who and how to buy bulk human hair. Selena loved everything about hair and learned every aspect of and about hair. If she didn't know it, she hired someone who did, and that was very, very rare because she was always teaching... be it life or hair.

A multitude of years later, some of her former employees have thanked her and admitted that not only did they work for her, but they were in class, studying as they worked, learning the art of a business woman. It's been said that to be imitated is the highest form of flattery. So many wanted to be like her, others would settle for just being in her presence. Clients came to Selena for expertise in hair weeving, but many, many of them enjoyed conversations with her. They obtained the wisdom that she would share with them.

Selena has this inner gift. She knows how to make a monster feel pretty and she can sprinkle enough confidence on the spirit of any bowed-down head that she has ever came in contact with in her line of business.

Selena taught her middle child, Juanita, and her youngest, her son, El, how to make up the hair (hand weft); her oldest daughter had a gift for doing hair. She was busy arching eyebrows, cutting and styling hair, building her own client base. This was the beginning stages of her teaching her children the importance and rewards of hard work, yet allowing her to keep a closer eye on them.

One day, Selena was in a panic and her mother, Mary, happened to be at the salon. Mary asked Selena what was wrong; why was she so upset. Selena responded by telling her mother that she had a client who wanted a weev, and though she had the hair, the hair was not wefted (made up). El and Juanita usually made up the hair, but were at school. She really didn't want to let this lady or her money walk out of the shop; $50.00 to $80.00 was a lot of money for a couple of hours of work back then.

Mary, whom Selena inherited her spirit of perseverance from, told Selena to show her what to do. The lady was being shampooed and prepped for Selena to work on, but Selena wasn't wasting anytime; she showed her mother how to loom the hair in a matter of minutes. By the time Selena escorted the client to her privately screened off area and completed one of the wefts, Mary had completely finished looming one piece of hair. Selena was happy, Mary was happy, and the client was happy to be able to receive such transforming results in one day.

Selena thanked her mother with a kiss and a hug; of course, she compensated her with money after she completed the client.

Meantime, a store became available in the next block, which was big enough for Selena to have her private office, including a twenty booth salon. Selena's House of Beauty was so busy people worked around the clock. The shop was open twenty-four hours; the staff worked in shifts.

Selena ordered more of the orange barber chairs and stools to match the custom made ones she had ordered previously.

Selena's House of Beauty and Hair Weev salon was jumping; it was a live party almost every day. The juke box was blasting the latest jams… the accessories man would be in there with his lap full of trays for display. It never mattered that he was in a wheel chair. He was somebody and he had an assistant. He had pretty jewelry, pretty earrings, rings, bracelets, necklaces and hosiery. The ladies wanted it, he supplied it, and they bought it. They may have had their outfit and shoes, but they always waited for him to help them complete their look.

The number runners would come through; everybody didn't play with the same person. Some played with this one, others might play with that one; some occasions some played double by playing with more than one runner. The pimps, the working girls and the boosters were still around for the move down the street, too; but no one had heard from Black Barry. Some of his girls were still working and some were trying to wait on him.

One pitiful girl was sitting in Selena's chair one day crying and worrying. When Selena asked her what was wrong, she replied through sniffles, "I don't know what to do… I ain't got anybody to give my money to."

And after replaying that ludicrous statement in her mind, Selena thought, "This is a fool here. Maybe I should tell my man to get this fool's money."

Instead of acting on her inner thoughts, Selena told the girl that she was too pretty and worked too hard to be looking for a nigga to give her money to. It seemed a shame that the girl had no real direction, no positive direction.

Selena had plenty of friends, both male and female. One guy, in particular, wanted to be more than friends. In fact, he turned out to be a stalker. Before he became a stalker, or before Selena actually realized that he was one, she didn't know it. Unfortunately, people could be watching you and you don't even realize it.

This man had offered to take her to dinner and a movie several times, but she always exclaimed how busy she was and thanked him for the offer. The man explained how he understood being busy, due to his busy schedule as a police officer. Although he claimed he understood, he remained very persistent. He came to her salon every day, inviting her out again and again. He told her he had been promoted to detective, therefore, wherever she wanted to go, he would take her. Selena finally accepted his invitation to dinner and a movie. They talked and laughed over dinner, just getting acquainted you know.

Upon arriving at the theatre, Selena noticed some things about her date that she hadn't noticed before. Two pet peeves that turned Selena off about a man are his shoes and socks. Actually, she has a couple of more no-nos when it comes to a man…broke is a third one, which is really number one. This man had two that she could plainly see in the well-lit lobby of the movie theatre. He had strings hanging out of his socks, you know when the elastic is failing and wants out and the socks refuse to stay up.

Oh, my goodness. Please don't let his ankles be ashy, she thought to herself…they were. To top that off, his shoes were ran over like a runner at a track meet, nonstop running over and over; he was almost walking on his ashy ankles. She hated it, but kept her cool. Once they were seated in the theatre she thought…well, he had a good job and he seemed nice, plus with his new promotion he could buy new shoes and socks. She made up in her mind not to look down at his feet anymore, and if she happened to forget, thankfully, it was dark in the theatre.

The man began eating the popcorn he had purchased for them to share; she didn't like the way he ate the popcorn. He would toss the popcorn way up in the air, lean his head far back enough to catch it with his mouth, and chew it with his mouth open. The noise he created from his little ritual was hideous to Selena, it was beyond smacking. She was turned all the way off by this time; she knew after he dropped her off that night, she wouldn't go anywhere else with him.

The "date from hell nightmare" began coming to the salon every day, claiming he was her man and she was his woman. She tried to be gentle with him because some people don't take rejection well at all. It hadn't been that long ago that that man on the Westside had chopped his wife's head off and took it to the neighborhood bar and told the bartender..."Give this B her last drink," as he set the head on top of the bar.

Selena explained the way this detective kept coming around, just sitting and watching any and everyone who talked to her, was not good for her business. She told him to stop coming to the shop. He listened and decided to sit out front in his car every day. Selena figured he would get the message soon and stop coming by period, until one day, as she was heading to her car, he jumped out of his and made her an offer. As usual she answered no again.

Chapter Twenty-Six

One night he told her they should get a place together, build a tall wall around it so no one could see them and they themselves wouldn't be able to see outside of it. They would stay in there together. Selena, still trying to maintain calm, was thinking to herself the whole time... *this nigga's truly crazy*. She asked him how they would live if they never left the premises. Of course, he had an answer; he would only go out when necessary for grocery.

Fed up with his deranged sense of romance, Selena told him for the umpteenth time that she did not want see him anymore. He refused to accept that. He began stalking her at home, which really unnerved both Selena and her mother, Mary. One day Mary arrived home from work to find that imbecile stretched out in the hallway of the building they lived in.

Mary didn't realize it was the man who had been stalking Selena. All she knew was that she was unable to get to the other inner door without stepping on him or over him.

"Excuse me," Mary said to the tall lanky man sprawled out on the floor with his back against the wall and his feet stretched out in front, touching the other wall. The maniac refused to move and told her that he was waiting for Selena.

Mary stepped over his long legs, went upstairs into their apartment and called Selena. Mary informed Selena that it was a crazy bastard in the hallway refusing to move or leave, saying he was waiting for her. For a brief moment, Selena was wondering who it was, but after Mary began describing...

"A tall crazy ass nigga with strings hanging from his socks and shoes running over!" Selena knew who it was.

Mary was upset and told Selena she was going to have to do something about him; call the police or something. Angry that he had now upset her mother, Selena went to the police station and spoke with some officers about him. She was leery about filing a complaint because he was an officer.

After telling them about the man and him being a detective, she explained that she was not trying to cause him to lose his job, but she wanted it clear that she wanted him to stay away from her, her home and her business. Selena left the station, hoping that some of his colleagues could convince him to leave her alone completely. After hearing Selena's story, the police decided to stake out the stalker. They put a squad car at her home and one at her business to see, if they could catch this fool in action.

When the officers caught him, they were shocked. They certainly knew him, but he was no officer of the law; he was a stoolie, a stool pigeon, an informant for the police. Selena could not believe her ears when the officers informed her of that. The real policemen promised her that he would not be a hindrance to her, her family or her business ever again. They warned him that he was to go nowhere near 63rd and Cottage and nowhere near her place of residence. I don't know what they had on him, but, after that, he did not violate their orders.

Days returned to normal, such as they were. As usual, never dull, the happenings were happening, money was flowing and anyone who wanted to make money was able to do so in those days. I remember a foreigner told me he came to this (our) country because of the open opportunities, which allow anyone to make money legally anywhere, anytime of day. That was a true statement, back in those times. The shoe shine boy (which was more times than not, a man) even made a good living. There were a number of other hustles and businesses. There were the policy owners, who had teams of number runners, and the vending machine owners who leased the most popular vending item... the juke box. The juke box would have all of the records that were hits on it. The juke boxes were placed in the lounges, beauty shops, barber shops and restaurants. In those days, if the business owners didn't own the juke box, they allowed the vendor to put it in their places of business for a cut of the profits.

One gentleman was new to Chicago and became a shoeshine boy at The House of Nelson's, but because of disagreements with the owner's wife, he was offered a spot in Selena's. Selena became like an older sister to him. They shared a passion for hustling and making money. He spoke so highly of Selena when he wrote or spoke to his mother back in St. Louis that when he decided to marry, his mother, who was a business woman herself, sent Selena the money for the groom and his bride.

He went from being a shoeshine boy to a numbers runner, to an assistant to the juke box man, to owning his own vending company. At that time, he was one of many getting their hustle on, and the money was flowing.

Selena had a new man, a successful business man, who loved to gamble and play golf. We'll just call him Mr. Money because he always had plenty of it and Selena spoke of him as one of her best friends because he would help in any way he could. Unless he was going to the golf course, he wore business attire every day. Whether he was wearing one of his tailor made suits with matching hat for his bald, extremely clean shaved head and shoes, or wearing his leisure wear that he wore on the golf course as he played, he gambled and talked trash with some other great movers and shakers. He was always well put together; even his socks matched. Mr. Money's staple accessory was a long fresh cigar, either in his hand or resting in his mouth. His appearance showed his love for the finer things in life in a big way, and he had deep pockets lined with silk to hold the big wads of money he carried.

Speaking of big, he had a long new blue Pontiac when they met and soon helped Selena purchase a convertible silver one. A short time later, maybe a week or so later, Selena turned the Pontiac in for something she wanted more…a silver convertible Cadillac Coup De Ville. As usual, when she arrived and parked in her usual parking spot, the men were hanging out and coming out of the various shops to admire her and her brand new car.

The men knew that her Pontiac was brand new, and they could not believe that this was her new Cadillac so they asked her whose car it was. She responded that it was hers.

During those days, most black people were happy to see their own people prosper. They had more pride in each other, which translated into inspiration.

Selena went on into work. A few hours later, Mr. Money came to visit his lady, but before he could go into the salon, the same men watched as he took a second look at the brand new "Kitty".

"Do you know who this car belongs to?" one of the men asked Money.

Mr. Money responded no. OMG, they couldn't wait to tell him that it was Selena's. Of course, he didn't believe them. He went in and walked straight to her office. When he got her alone, he screamed, "Is That Your Car?"

She told him, "Yes." She tried to ask him did he like it, but after he heard yes, he lost it.

"WHAT YOU DOING WITH..."

"HOW YOU GONE..."

"WHO GONE PAY FOR IT"?

"YOU!!!!" she snapped

Within a week, he traded his blue Pontiac for a brand new light blue Cadillac.

From then, on they both purchased a new Cadillac every year, neither of them ever kept their cars over two years. Mr. Money would buy Broughams, but Selena would switch it up a bit over the years, buying Coupes, Broughams and Eldorados. Some were convertible. Others had sun/moon roofs.

Money and Selena enjoyed a loving, fun-filled and exciting courtship for quite a while. Money romanced her with expensive outings in and out of state. They were always going out to fancy dinners, eating his favorite "Filet Mignon" steaks. Selena has always been a chicken and dressing girl, however, she enjoyed the rich atmosphere of the elegant restaurants they traveled to.

Many times, Money would have his driver drive them to Florida, to the Fountain Bleu Hotel. Money loved to play golf everywhere, but he especially loved playing on the greens in Florida. While Money would golf with many of the big timers, one of which was Heavy Weight Champion, Joe Louis, Selena would sometime slip away to do some shopping. One particular time, she went into an upscale shoe store. She noticed the white sales ladies, though reluctant, waited on her. Selena could see and feel their hateful disapproval in every expression of their faces, as well as in every move they made.

With her signature smile and a twinge of nervousness in her stomach, she continued to request to try shoe after shoe. With each pair, the sales women grew more and more irritated, thinking she couldn't afford one pair of them. Selena took great joy in leaving them with their mouths hanging open wide enough for a bird to fly into each one of them… she bought ten pairs of shoes. Most of them were for her, of course, but a few were for her two daughters and her mother.

That wouldn't be the only time Selena would experience the still coldness of racism while traveling with Money. One time, in particular stuck out in her mind; it was the time they were riding down the highway, on the outskirts of Florida, chauffeur-driven of course. They decided that they were hungry and informed the driver to pull in to this restaurant just off the highway.

Upon doing so, they realized it was a drive-in type of restaurant and waited for the waiter to come to the car. Shortly after, a tall dark handsome black man approached their big, pretty shiny Cadillac. He knelt down and peered through the open window with his beautiful bright smile and asked, "What can I do for you folks?"

Before they could answer, he realized they were colored, Negroes. He stood straight up as if he were called to attention by a superior officer, turned his back to their car and his lips were sealed with fear… not a tooth was showing.

Selena and Money spent about a minute trying to place their order with the young man, but he kept his back to them with no response. While Money was questioning the young man, wondering what was wrong with the man and why he wouldn't respond, Selena fell silent, but, at the same time, she experienced heartache and disappointment.

Only when Money began to cuss at the man for continuing to ignore their request did Selena release her silence. Selena, with an apparent lack of energy, interrupted Money, as she told him that she was no longer hungry. She had lost her appetite. She told Money, they should just leave because it wasn't the man's fault.

Selena figured out something. Though the man was a Negro, too, he was not allowed to serve his own kind. His boss did not serve colored folks. They were only good enough to work there—not to eat there. Selena felt empathy for him; she could feel his motionless emotions were based on fear. What she imagined he was feeling was racing through her mind. She imagined that he thought if he had taken their order, although it was dark outside and his boss may have not seen that they were colored, he would lose his job. He could not take the chance of being unable to put food on his own table by losing his job, being banned from working anywhere in the area, physically harmed or worse—forced to leave his hometown had anyone seen them and told the boss he had served them.

Suddenly, Selena, Mr. Money, and his driver had lost their appetites. They didn't stop again until they arrived at their hotel. Though they ended up enjoying themselves during the remainder of their trip that night of events remained in their minds for a lifetime.

After many more exciting getaways, nights out on the town, Selena and Money's romance was interrupted. One day one of Selena's operators informed her about a phone call they had answered earlier. There was a lady on the phone asking was her husband there. The operator asked the lady who her husband was and the lady responded, "Wilson"."

No one knew anyone by that name. The woman then asked for Wilson by his street name Money, which I choose to change as well as his first name and a few others in the book out of respect for everyone involved.

Upon the completion of the disappointing message, though shocked, Selena maintained her cool as she thanked the messenger. She went into her private office and spent some time alone as she changed into her uniform. Moments later, she took a deep breath, squared her shoulders, put her winning smile on and called for her first client.

After that, the relationship between Selena and Mr. Money had changed. It was over as he knew it. When she confronted him about his marriage, he was genuinely sorry, but sorry couldn't fix it. The damage was done, the trust was broken, completely breeched.

Nonetheless, Selena didn't wallow in the sorrow. Instead, she took the lesson as another confirmation that no matter what a woman may or may not do, a woman would never match the dirty deeds that most men pull off.

True enough, Mr. Money was sad, and it was no secret that he loved Selena. Even his wife realized how much he loved Selena. Love is a powerful emotion; it can make you lose all of your common sense, depending on your constitution, it can make you lose weight or cause you to gain weight. Those are just a few of the side effects that one could experience while engaged in the emotion of love. Mr. Money was so torn up about Selena ending their relationship, the love that his wife had for him allowed her to feel sorry for him because he was in such emotional distress. He wasn't mean to his wife; it's just that his heart and mind was always on Selena.

Chapter Twenty-Seven

✣

Selena was now a free agent again. It took some time, but Mr. Money bounced back to his old money-making jolly self after a while, and he and Selena remained friends until his transition. No matter whom he or she had, they were respectful friends for life.

One day, while preparing for one of her outstanding hair shows at Robert's Show Lounge, she reflected back on the first time Mr. Money told her that he loved her. Selena had started wearing a long beautiful pony tail with a curved bang. The first time Mr. Money saw her new look was a couple of days before a show, but that particular evening, they were on their way to dinner and a movie, and he felt that her shapely figure and sexy walk incited enough attention he didn't want her to receive any more attention.

"You don't need that shit on your head," he told Selena.

Selena asked him, *"You don't like it?"* but before he could respond, she blurted out, "Well, I Do!"

To her surprise, Mr. Money had snatched her pony tail, but it would not come off because it was weeved on. Much more to his surprise Selena had twirled around and had her two fingers, the index and middle fingers hooked inside both of his nostrils so fast, he immediately released her ponytail. Shocked by her nerve to retaliate and the severity of the pain of his nose, he surrendered and told her that he loved her.

He actually admired her for setting him straight on who the boss was concerning what she wore. Although he was "The Man" inside, outside and around town, his name was known all over the streets and his reputation was money. Mr. Money was not a woman abuser, and Selena knew he would never physically hurt her.

Though the thought brought a smile to her face, she shook the thought of him from her mind as she continued to prepare for her upcoming show.

Selena continued to focus on her business, not only was she producing hair and fashion shows for which her good friend, Vester, a millinery expert, provided her custom designed hats, she also participated in the annual Bud Billiken Parade.

Selena and a car full of some of her prettiest clients, including her daughters, would float through the parade in and on her convertible Cadillac. All of the ladies commanded attention with show-stopping, perfectly-dressed hair; some in custom-fitted dresses, some in swim suits, while others were in couture Bermuda shorts with silk blouses. Those that could not fit inside of the "Kitty," would ride on the hood of the car and the trunk of the car. Whether they wore pumps or slip on mules (bare backs), they were all gorgeous and sexy. She participated in that parade for several years.

Selena traveled to hair shows in other cities and states, which brought to the attention of "The Beauty Trade Magazine." On more than one occasion, Selena was featured as a stylist and a hair weev expert in photo shoots. One time, the crew from Beauty Trade came to Chicago to feature Selena as she curled an entire head of hair, which varied in lengths, with the same iron. They were particularly interested in her curling the shortest hair which was in the nape area without changing the iron. The curls were perfectly croquignoled from front to back, top to bottom all without any fishhooks and without burning the client/ model.

Another time was when Beauty Trade was very interested in this new thing...the art of "Hair Weev Technology."

The photographer took before and after pictures of Selena's model and the color, as well as the style from beginning to end were given in detail for copy in the magazine. Selena often advertised on the radio station "WVON". 'VON was the voice of the Negro. All of the best music would be heard on that station all day and all night. James Brown, Aretha Franklin, Gladys Knight & The Pips, Marvin Gaye, Tammi Terrell, The Supremes, The Temptations known as "The Temps," The Four Tops, Stevie Wonder, Isley Brothers and so many more could be heard during the day.

The Gospel greats were played, as well as the Blues greats like B.B. King, Bobby Blue Bland, Muddy Waters, Howling Wolf and too many more to name. WVON was to Black homes and businesses in Chicago what Ebony and Jet magazines were—a staple.

There were two to three books on the family coffee/ cocktail table. They were the Bible, Ebony and sometimes the Jet. Most times, the Jet would be in the kitchen, the bathroom or the bedroom, but it was there somewhere. I will always love Mr. Johnson for launching his great magazines. He was the very first to show the world that BLACK is beautiful and cover page worthy. He was proud of his people and their accomplishments, be it through talent, philanthropy, politics, hope or hell. Mr. Johnson had the nerve to print the good and the bad, the triumphs and the trials.

I love his wife, Eunice Johnson, for caring enough for women of color to launch a make-up and skin care line, Fashion Fair, designed especially for us. Most make-up lines cater to women of lighter expression (white), if they have any foundation or powder color of a somewhat deeper or darker shade in their line at all, it's usually only one. Well, that may be fine for the lightest women of color, which may be considered white chocolate. However, Mrs. Johnson was wise and considerate enough to accommodate skin tones from white chocolate to dark chocolate, and every shade in between. Anything less would never work for the many different shades of black beauty.

Back to WVON, Selena's advertisement was usually heard during the blues show hosted by Pervis Span, "The Blues Man." For years, Selena advertised with Mr. Span weekly. Mr. Span would play the recorded advertisement for Selena's, and then he would ad lib a bit longer by announcing that Selena could put hair on anything and anyone. He would say, "Selena can put hair on an onion!"

Selena continued to advertise her business and build her name brand for decades to come through various media outlets. Television, radio, newspapers, magazines and the "Yellow Pages" were most ways she would keep her brand on the consumers' minds, but her most important channel of advertisement was through the quality of service she and her staff provided, which created a stream of compliments and word-of-mouth recommendations from satisfied customers.

Word also spread about who may try to pursue Selena next. This particular time, still in the early sixties, there was a nice slightly older lady named Eunice who would come to the shop to have her hair done. In the course of time, she befriended Selena. Eunice happened to have had a nephew, whom was considered quite a catch…single, successful, and not bad looking.

Eunice would tell Selena how all of the women on the Westside wanted her nephew and how they were just throwing themselves at him, to no avail. After months of conversation with Eunice, Selena told the aunt maybe she needed to meet him. His aunt was thrilled because she had been trying to get Selena to meet him anyway.

Consequently, Selena agreed to meet the aunt and her husband at this popular lounge on the Westside. The "Caldonia" lounge was owned by Eunice's nephew, Joe. That was just one of his businesses; Joe also owned a Chinese restaurant across the street from his lounge. Selena sat at the bar with his aunt and uncle, ordered her usual glass of orange juice and enjoyed the music, the conversation, and the company while waiting to be introduced.

Joe, a short man, with a close cropped haircut (which was prevalent back then for men that didn't wear a process) with a brown complexion (he was neither dark or light, but a medium color that my grandfather would refer to as "Pretty Brown" when he spoke to my mother, his daughter and any other female with that caramel color complexion;) in fact, there were several similarities in him and my grandfather such as their height, the color of their skin, and their habitual thirst for a "taste."

Joe came into his lounge with a big grin on his face, glad to see his business profiting as usual. Glasses were being filled and refilled, people were dancing to the sounds on the juke box and money was flowing. Joe's aunt motioned with a wave of her hand for her nephew to come to the end of the bar where she, his uncle and Selena were seated.

Gliding through the crowd, shaking hands along the way, Joe greeted his aunt and uncle with hugs as they made small talk jokes. Joe and Selena were introduced and seemed to hit it off right away. Joe invited Selena to his restaurant for a bite to eat. They got acquainted over Chinese food.

After that, Joe invited Selena to the restaurant and the lounge quite often, and she would go. He would sometimes pick her up and they would go out, as well. It was a short courtship. In no time at all, they were married.

Joe didn't drink a lot during their courtship; he wined and dined her almost every night while dating her. Whatever she liked, whatever she wanted, he would get it for her.

For instance, Selena loved fried fish.

One night Joe brought home the most delicious fried Buffalo fish. They had a good time eating it. However, the next week, he brought home raw fresh fish to be cleaned and cooked by Selena. Needless to say, Selena had been working all day in her salon and was very tired, so when she saw the fish was raw after she opened the package she grabbed her Pepsi and packet of peanuts and jumped in the bed.

That was the first argument the newlyweds had. During the six months of courting, Joe had not paid attention that Selena had never prepared one meal for him. She worked too hard. Besides, he always took her out to eat.

Once her children were able to fix themselves something to eat and her mother was there to cook, Selena had traded in her kitchen stove for her salon stoves, which were used for cooking hair, not food. Selena's mother, Mary, enjoyed cooking and catering so she cooked most of the meals at Selena's home.

By this time, her daughters had both had children and were in their respective apartments. Her son was the only other mouth she had to feed at that time, and if he didn't eat with his mother at the shop, he ate what his grandmother, Mary, had cooked at home.

There was a reason Selena had waited so many years to marry after her divorce. Selena had never wanted to marry any man while her daughters were still at home with her. Not only did she not want a man over them, she did not want to have to worry about any type of abuse towards them.

I am her first grandchild. As a child growing up, my grandmother seemed bigger than life to me.

She always had such a pretty smile and smelled so good. The way she looked in her clothes, the way she looked in her tailor-made clothes was star time. She was, and still is, classy superstar quality. I mean, if Hollywood had been in Chicago, she would have been a serious staple in it. However, she has always been a trend setter and a staple among Chicago's elite.

Although they were still newlyweds, Joe had begun to reveal his true self. He would often drink himself silly, especially on occasions that Selena would want him to purchase something for her. Like the time she wanted a new car, a Cadillac, of course, because that's what she liked, and a Cadillac is what she drove. When she and Joe met, Selena was driving a convertible "hog"… that was one of the street names for the "Caddi." There were several nicknames for the Cadillac, depending on how it was decked out how it looked and how it made people feel.

Some people say a Cadillac purrs like a kitten, thus the "Caddi" became the "Kitty." The sleek quiet engine, not to mention the luxury inside and out of a Cadillac, was the introduction and seduction of cruising on dry land. I mean it was like floating down the street, and still is to this day.

Even back then in the early 60s, Selena was treated like royalty. The Cadillac dealer would send the salesman with the new Cadillac to her home for her to inspect. Selena had two salesmen, Mr. Mass and Mr. Stein, who she always dealt with, and they knew her taste. They always knew what Selena would like, and they would send it to her home for her to check it out. If she liked it, liked what she saw, she would keep it. If not, she would go into the dealership to pick something she really liked.

This time when they brought the car to the house, she was married to Joe and he was so drunk, it was embarrassing.

Joe yelled with his thick tongue, "What They Bring That Here for?"

"Me!" Selena answered. "I'm getting a new car!"

Joe stumbled a bit as he tried to stand straight up and put his foot down. He clowned, he ranted and raved that he was not going to pay for a new Cadillac right now. "I need time to think about it!" he exclaimed. Selena, embarrassed by his actions, but not deterred, told the salesman to leave the car there. Of course, Selena bought the car. It was a pretty red convertible, Coupe Deville with a black top. Inside was smooth black leather interior.

Selena didn't have to pay any bills at the home she and Joe shared; she worked hard enough that she felt she deserved anything she wanted. Unfortunately, Joe's drinking and tight-fisted cheapness started taking a toll on Selena and their marriage; it prompted her to go and speak with a lawyer. Attorney Einhorne advised Selena of the pros and cons of dissolving the marriage at that time. He advised Selena that if she expected anything from the marriage that she would have to remain married for at least a year. Incidentally, Mr. Einhorne remained Selena's lawyer from that day until the day he died. Mr. Einhorne was one of her key advisers in both personal and business decisions.

Chapter Twenty-Eight

For the remainder of the year, Selena stuck it out, enduring Joe's drinking, and the bickering. Just as the year was passing, or shall I say coming to a close, so was their marriage. While arguing yet again, Selena chose this opportunity to execute her exit strategy. Selena could not take another day of his drinking and arguing so instead of ignoring him like she would normally do, she heightened the argument by taking it to the next level.

After her first divorce from my grandfather, wherever she lived, her mother lived with her. Usually when Selena and Joe would argue, they would try to keep it to a minimum because of Mary's living with them, but how often can you argue in a low tone? Mary never interfered when they argued, but this time there was a loud smack and Selena screamed! Selena was crying and screaming, "You hit me, you hit me!"

Her mother, Mary, was in there within seconds with her signature weapon, a butcher's knife, prepared to turn Joe into a filet. Selena didn't want that on her hands. She was able to give her mother the "eye" and let her know that Joe had not really hit her and everything was okay, without letting him or his family know. However, as far as they and the police were concerned, he had hit her.

I have mixed emotions about that myself. I understand wanting to get out of a bad marriage and the abuse may not have been physical, but mental and verbal abuse can be just as bad and sometimes worse. Constant arguing and bickering can be draining to the body and spirit, and Selena refused to live another day like that, but I have brothers, and I would hate to see them tricked like that. However, if they behaved in that manner, drinking and arguing, arguing and drinking, day after day, I suppose it could warrant desperate measures to be relieved of that torment.

I'm really glad there was no bloodshed and that my great-grandmother was not sent to jail before I had the pleasure of knowing herJ.

That little farce helped in granting Selena her divorce, which yielded a nice settlement that allowed Selena to purchase her first property with a sizable down payment in the affluent Chatham area of Chicago. It was an all brick, two- flat beautiful building with a three-bedroom apartment up over a store front. The store became the home of Selena's House of Beauty and School of Hair Weev* Technology. A new beginning!

Selena had combined both her Pershing hotel and Mansfield hotel salons into the 6318 S. Cottage location, now she divided the staff in half again, establishing Selena's House of Beauty 2 at the 83rd St. Salon in Chatham. This came right on time. There were many changes taking place. Cottage Grove was, quote unquote, drying up so to speak. Prostitutes, boosters, even pimps and number runners were harassed and arrested from time to time, but the last time that they loaded all the prostitutes into the paddy wagon, Selena said she almost wanted to get in there with them. Of course, she felt bad for them but she felt worse for her, her business and her employees because that was their money rolling away…some of it anyway. A lot of them had become like friends of Selena's House of Beauty. They were there on a regular basis, which was often daily.

When they came to Selena's, they were treated like every other client. They could laugh, share stories, and leave out, looking better and feeling better; they didn't feel condemned when they came to Selena's.

That's one thing I'm proud of. I don't come from a close minded family. We were taught to respect everyone. We meaning my brothers, a cousin and I were exposed to all types of people while growing up in our grandmother's salons. Some became lifelong family friends and some more like aunts and uncles who helped nurture and teach us along the way. Many of them were gay, and we loved every bit of them!

I found out later, as I became an adult, what was the norm for us, was quite different for some others. As I became an adult, a young adult, not many, but a few people would gather up the nerve to ask me questions pertaining to gay people, especially the ones that worked for my grandmother. Questions like, "How could you stand to be around them? How could you eat their food?" They asked these type of things, as well as many other degrading questions and comments that assured me that they themselves had led a very sheltered life.

Most likely, it probably wasn't their fault entirely that their parents hadn't been able to explain to them that there are differences in people, but that doesn't make them any less or better than you. To simplify things even more is less judgment. There are many different lifestyles in the world, and I feel, unless a person is a serious criminal like a serial killer, a murderer, a sex offender or a pedophile, they are not doing anything to hurt anyone else. If anything, the only one that usually gets hurt, especially back in those days, is the gay person themselves, by homophobic individuals who let their fear supersede their common sense.

My response to them and those that would ask me those questions and make those nasty comments is that you don't know what you're missing! No I don't eat from everyone. There are some heterosexuals who can't cook, and if they could, I wouldn't eat their food. But when you're able to find a good cook, a good tailor, a good whatever needs to be done person, they usually have followers and that was way before twitter or Face book, often called the in crowd. Now if you find a cook, a hair stylist, a domestic cleaner, a clothing designer, an interior designer etc. who happens to be gay and that is their passion, whatever their passion is, they can do that to the hundredth power times ten. The nines would not do. Whatever they do, they do their best and usually do it well!

Chapter Twenty-Nine

I remember since I've been grown, a lady came into the shop who was a former employee of my grandmother's salon and she shared a story with me. She informed me that before she worked for my grandmother, she was working in another salon down the street from my grandmother's salons. She went on to explain how she and her fellow coworkers would laugh and talk about my grandmother for having all of those gay people in her salon, but she admitted that they themselves had become the joke because Selena's House of Beauty's door was constantly swinging, opening and closing, opening and closing, busy all the time.

As time went on, the stylists from down the street had very few clients. Most of the time, the only ones looking in their mirrors were she and her coworkers themselves. One thing they noticed, she said, Selena always had a smile on her face, and she and her fellow haters had figured out why… she was laughing all the way to the bank. That was why this former employee came to work for Selena.

My grandmother was there listening and smiling, when the former employee got to that part of her story, Selena let out a hardy "AMEN!" Selena revealed that she and her coworkers would have wastebaskets full of money. Many times they were so busy, the pockets on their uniforms weren't deep enough to hold the money for the day. The wastebaskets were a good hiding spot for a while, but soon Selena would have to buy a cash register, and she was the only one with the key. I remember the big green machine with the long handle (It really was green).

I'll never forget, as a child, when she taught me how to work it…. Oh, my God! I thought that was really something, pushing the buttons, pulling the handle, watching and listening to the sound of the cash drawer open was fascinating.

What was even more mesmerizing was, if you didn't have the key inserted and the knob in the correct position that drawer would not open. That was back in the sixties. I know the world has come a long way, baby, but that was during the days when, unless you were a pretty big business. Your cash register was a cigar box, a coffee can or a wastebasket. I was even in awe of my grandmother's keys. She had the biggest bunch of keys, and I always wanted to have a lot of keys. To me, it meant you had something.

Selena, a young grandmother now, moved into her new building with her mother, Mary, and her son, Elmer, Junior, who was affectionately called Al until he changed it to El. By now, Selena's two daughters were young mothers themselves and had their own apartments.

I remember, as a small child, living only minutes away from the shops on Cottage Grove at 64th and Maryland. However, when my grandmother, great-grandmother and uncle moved to Chatham, my mother moved us as well.

We were only minutes away again on 80th and Maryland. My mother always loved to be close to her mother. She could get to work easier. It made it easier for us to be picked up from school and enabled us to come to the shop right after school, in case my mother wasn't through working. As a result, we were always enrolled in a school right near the shop.

Although one year I was enrolled in Sabarbraro Grade School, currently known as Arthur Ashe School, which was closer to our apartment, and a few years later, when my mother and stepfather, Herbert, had our home built on 92nd street, we did a year at Burnside School. We always ended back at Dixon grade school, which is where we all graduated from.

Meantime, Selena was working her plan and planning her work. She was putting her name on the map, constantly and continuously enhancing her brand with a zealous diligence, which brought her decades of success. Over the years, she shared her success with her family, not only her mother and children, but her younger sister worked with her for short time as well. And when we, her grandchildren, became old enough, we were taught her craft and the importance of hard work, as well.

For Selena, being the beautiful, sexy, successful woman she was, romance was never far away. This time it came in the form of a minister, a recent divorced man, whose wife had moved their three children back to Detroit. Reverend JA Williams had been called to preach at Mount Zion Missionary Baptist Church on the Southside of Chicago. Reverend JA Williams served as the Minister of Mount Zion for a few years, which is where he was pastor when he met Selena. Actually, he had met Selena a couple of years before while visiting her salon on Cottage Grove with a female acquaintance of his, who happened to be a gospel singer, but he never forgot Selena.

Jay didn't have a lot of materialistic things, but he had that special something that today they call "swagger." After giving up his house, he had a little beige four-door Plymouth, a few suits and an apartment. However, Jay was a staunch reader, which made him very articulate and intelligent. His ministerial skills were off the charts. Could he preach? Could Ali box?

Absolutely, for sure yes to both questions. Jay was able to wine and dine Selena, engross her in clever conversation, while making her feel as if she was the only woman on earth for him.

Reverend Williams, being the profound, handsome preacher, whose attire became emphatically better due to the company he was keeping, had women chasing after him all of the time, as did Selena have men fantasizing and hoping for a chance with her. They made a beautiful couple. Their winning personalities combined with their energetic and successful business minds and down-to-earth personas created a magnetic aura individually, but, as a couple, it was beautiful fireworks.

They were having fun as a couple, but they decided to take it slow and enjoy each other's company. It was hardly all play time. They worked diligently to make their dreams come true. Selena had dreams of opening a salon in the Chicago Loop area so she and her fellow colleague and good friend Ms. Rogers, who had a hair weev* salon in Maywood, opened their salon together in the Stephen's building downtown at 17 N. State Street.

That was quite an accomplishment, due to there not being many, in fact very few black businesses in the Chicago Loop, especially black-owned beauty salons that provided services for all genders while catering to all ethnic backgrounds. By this time Selena had moved the 63rd street location to the 83rd street and combined the two salons. Selena worked in the loop salon on Tuesday and Thursday, allowing her to work in her Southside salon the rest of the week Wednesday Friday and Saturday, while Ms. Rogers worked in the loop on Wednesday and Friday they would usually alternate Saturdays.

They both had fully staffed salons at their individual main locations, including their children who were fully qualified to service clients in their absence. This, in turn, enabled those staff members, including their children to build their own clientele.

Selena and Ms. Rogers would travel to various cities to participate in trade shows, meeting up with other colleagues of the beauty culture and the small circle of hair weavers. Shows such as, the Allied Cosmetology Association, the National Beauty Culture League Association, and the world renowned Bronner Brothers beauty and tradeshow in Atlanta, Georgia.

While some of them were just colleagues, many of them became close friends and staunch supporters of each other. I remember, as a small child, attending an Allied cosmetology Association meeting with my grandmother. I believe it was at the Baptist Institute on King Drive., which was South Park back then in the early 60s. I believe it was a Monday morning around 10 A.M. That's when women used to really dress. None of them had on pants; they all wore beautiful suits.

Some had on hats to match, but I have to tell the truth. My grandmother was always the one to stand out in the room. No matter how crowded, she always made an entrance and got the second and third looks because she was always the sharpest.

However, that day, a little girl was impressed with all of the ladies in that room. I don't remember all of their names, but I remember some. There was Mary Hanna, Maggie Burton, Ms. Oliver, my grandmother, Selena, and Ms. Isabel Joseph Johnson.

All of those ladies, including the ones that I don't remember their names, were dressed to the nines for business, had their own businesses and had come together as a united front in order to enhance their capabilities as black businesswomen of the city of Chicago. Believe it or not, hairstylists, designers and hair weave technicians are powerful resources. They create and set trends that the rest of the world of women follow and trust.

At the time, Isabel Joseph Johnson had her own television show, "Rock of Ages," on Channel 26 and she was a personality on WVON radio station. She and Bernadine C. Washington were the only two ladies on WVON with "The Good Guys."

To see Ms. Johnson in the flesh after seeing her on Channel 26 every Saturday evening and listening to her on various commercials on WVON, such as Archi B's, was like WOW!! And she knew my grandmother and my grandmother knew her was a double WOW!

Pretty soon Ms. Rogers grew tired of traveling back and forth to the city, so she bowed out of the downtown location with Selena. The downtown location was booming and Selena was in no ways tired. In fact, she moved into a larger unit in the Stephen's building.

However, Jay was growing tired of being told what he could and could not do as pastor of the Mount Zion Missionary Baptist Church. He began making plans to found his own church.

After discussing it with Selena and a few of his close associates, he received answered prayers of strong encouragement. He resigned from Mount Zion and, one evening, in the basement of Selena's house of beauty at 444 E. 83rd St., the Greater Monumental Missionary Baptist Church was founded by the Reverend JA Williams, along with Selena, Jay's good friend, Reverend Dickerson, and about eight other members.

Meantime, Selena and Jay had been dating seriously for about two years. Things were moving along. They were growing as a couple. Their businesses were growing. Everything they touched was working out for the good to them that love God. After another year or so, they decided to get married.

Even though they had found a store front church to house Greater Monumental on 76th and Halsted, they planned for the wedding to be held in First Church of Deliverance. Although there were many people happy to hear of the glowing couple's anticipated nuptials, there were a few people that were highly disappointed and against the future wedding. Ironically, all of the naysayers in the grapevine kept their negative opinions in the grapevine.

Even her good longtime friend, Mr. B.B. King, wrote her closest friend, Vester, a letter, begging her to tell him it wasn't true and please don't let that happen. He went as far as to ask Vester to ask Selena not to do it. Mr. King and Selena never had an argument, never had a falling out. There was a time when they spent quite a bit of time together. I think it's safe to say they loved each other.

In fact, when I told him that I was writing a book several years ago that was the one thing he told me I could say. "I love your grandmother and I love you," he said one night after one of his legendary performances. I know they have the utmost respect for one another, by the way they speak of one another. I remember the first time Selena told me B.B. King had wrote a song about her called "Beautician Blues." I was so surprised!

Chapter Thirty

There was a time Selena hosted a birthday party for B.B. King and her mother, Mary, catered it for him. His band and a few others were invited. My mother even remembers that. The most pleasant surprise of all was me going with Selena to see B. B. King perform for the first time. I was excited and nervous. Although I knew Selena had never lied to me, I was wondering were we really going to be able to go backstage to see him. When we arrived, she asked to see him and gave her name. That person let the right people know and his road manager came out with this huge grin on his face and greeted Selena with a hug.

"Hey, how have you been?" he said as he led us to Mr. King.

B.B. was thrilled to see Selena. They greeted one another with a warm gentle embrace. Just as they were about to take a seat, he asked "Who is this?" in a curious but gentle tone.

"That's Bonnie!" she informed him.

"That's Bonnie? Last time I saw her she was a little bitty baby."

"That's Bonnie," she reiterated. We shook hands and hugged.

Since that time, it became a ritual for Selena and I to go and see B.B. King whenever he came in town.

For many, many years, me being the youngster, I would ride as my grandmother, Selena, drove us, but such as life would have it, as she became older, she would ride and I became the driver.

Some of the best times of being backstage with the King of the Blues, which they were all phenomenal, but the times I really loved were the times when Mr. King would give us youngsters a history lesson. Sharing who he grew up listening to and what inspired him about that particular artist. He would also share a new gadget that he was listening to music and his icons on.

At that particular time, it was one of the smallest recording devices I had ever seen or heard of. No, I don't remember all of the artists he spoke about. It's been so long ago, but I cherish being in Mr. King's "history class" for those moments in time. I learned never to forget your roots, but to be open and receptive to new and exciting things.

As I said earlier, they never had a cross word between them. It's just that their careers took them on different paths. Mr. B.B. King has always been such a nice man, a real gentleman. Although I am not his granddaughter, there were plenty of times he treated me like I was and I thank him.

Vester finally showed Selena Mr. King's letter, but it was too late. The wedding plans were in motion. The wedding took place at First Church of Deliverance on 43rd and Wabash and Reverend Clarence H. Cobb performed the ceremony. I heard the wedding was beautiful.

I missed the wedding because I was with my aunt, whom was usually late, and my cousin, in the store getting shoes for the finishing touch of our outfits that we were to wear to the wedding. We did make it to the reception, which was held at the shop in the basement, and in the back yard. Well, really all over the shop. People were allowed upstairs in the apartment to see the new renovations that had recently been done for the festivities.

However, they didn't stay long because my great-grandmother Mary was on patrol.

I remember her saying, "I will be up here. I've got to watch these whores. They won't be able to steal nothing or plant nothing."

The kitchen was completely gutted and remodeled with new fixtures and appliances. All furniture that was not new was reupholstered. New carpet and the living room wall was mirrored from floor to ceiling. Every room was exquisite. What a party it was! It was awesome! The entire day of events was Hollywood Chicago-style, just as many other future events that Selena hosted would be. My grandmother had changed from her beautiful powder blue wedding gown and matching veil to what looked like a complete diamond dress. It was a silk dress completely covered in clear rhinestones and crystals. It was beautiful.

Someone—I believe it was one of her clients—had given her a silky terrier as a wedding gift. The dog's name was Yogi. She was a golden blonde Yorkie, with little touches of silver. She became very attached and protective of Selena.

Yogi was very comfortable being carried around in my grandmother's arms at the reception and for the duration of her life. I mean for years, Yogi was carried around with her head held up as she sat cradled in my grandmother's arms, as if she knew she was a princess being carried by a queen. That little dog truly acted as though she and Selena were royalty and off limits to the rest of us. If anyone knocked on my grandmother's office door, got too close to her car door, attempted to invade the boundaries surrounding my grandmother's personal space, it was a no-no. Yogi would clown. She would attack the door, running into it back and forth while barking and growling.

Even though Yogi wasn't much bigger than a football that could have been kicked for a touchdown, no one ever did kick her.

I was afraid of her and her teeth. When I was a younger child, I witnessed firsthand how serious a dog's love was, especially how dogs love their master.

Years before Yogi, my grandmother had the most beautiful black and tan pure breed German shepherd. Lucky was his name. Lucky was more of a family dog. He belonged to Selena, my Uncle El and my great-Grandmother Mary.

Selena named her new puppy, Lucky, because she said he had to be Lucky for her to purchase him for her and my Uncle El, and for her to make the commitment to embark on the added responsibility it takes to be a pet owner. Not only was Lucky the prettiest German shepherd, he had been to obedience school, which made him extremely obedient and smart. One other person, Lucky, was obedient with was Sid, one of Selena's operators in the shop. Sid loved to walk Lucky and Lucky loved Sid.

However, Lucky really loved my grandmother, Selena, and would get a little jealous when she bestowed affection toward anyone else, but unlike Yogi, Lucky was quiet with his disapproval. One evening, while my grandmother Selena was relaxing in her sky blue chaise lounge, I was up there with her. I was with her a lot. Whenever there was a chance for me to be around my grandmother, I was there.

This particular evening, she was hugging me and talking baby talk, just showing me some love when one of my hands was stuck behind my back exposing my thumb. Well, Lucky eased around to the side of the chaise that I was on and bit my thumb! He knew better than to bite me real hard, but he bit me hard enough for me to understand his language. That bite meant GET UP! I did, but my grandmother made him feel so ashamed he actually went and hid in another room. She told him she could not believe he bit me.

"Bonnie," she went on to say, "Bonnie is our baby."

Lucky ran and hid. Pets can be possessive, too, but, I doubt if my grandmother would have been able to shame a pit bull into hiding. What a different world we live in. Dogs are not just family pets anymore. A lot of them are now killers. Some are trained that way and some have that instinct naturally. People rarely argue or fight anymore; they kill each other. People! Be Strong and wise enough to walk away. It's okay to take the high road, "If it means staying above ground."

Now let's get back to the country girl with the magical, gifted and skillful hands. Not only did she work wonders and perform a few miracles, but everything she put her mind to became a success.

Selena and Jay continued to work and plan. They soon moved into the storefront at 7541 S. Halsted. They were always networking and campaigning for new members. Selena's House of Beauty was a great avenue for reaching out to people and it did produce quite a few members.

However, they also hosted quite a few small gatherings, such as dinner parties at the house, or meetings at the church with ministers and musicians alike, which led to many long-term relationships that were bred out of fellowships. Oh, they were growing, both Greater Monumental Missionary Baptist Church and Selena's House of Beauty.

Chapter Thirty-One

It wasn't hard for them to get into the fellowship circle because as a Minister, a preacher, a shepherd, Reverend JA Williams had wonderful interpersonal skills. He was a phenomenal speaker, yet he could make his message plain. Also, another plus factor was that people loved to see them coming. They always looked so sharp, so polished and so together. Even as a couple, they had charisma. It was like a fashion show every time they entered a church, a ballroom, a restaurant, a funeral home. Whatever and wherever, they did not disappoint. A lot of people even tried to emulate them. Those that could not emulate them admired them, while some just wanted to be with them. There were many ministers and preachers who wanted a first lady like Selena, well-dressed, classy, first and foremost, always a lady.

Jay really enjoyed introducing her as his wife. It became a ritual. If he was running a revival or a guest speaker at another church, just after giving thanks and honor to God, he would have his lovely wife to stand and he would introduce her to the congregation. Most of the people, especially women, knew of Selena from her reputation as a business woman, specializing in hair care and hair weeving*.

The membership and ministry at Greater Monumental continued growing. The members were enjoying being fed the word of God under the leadership of Reverend Williams. He developed a great rapport with his members.

It wasn't always easy, but my grandmother and Jay would even take my brother, my cousin, and myself to church with them every Sunday. I guess to make sure it was some bodies in the building at first. Eventually, though, word spread and hard work and perseverance paid off. It was truly a combination of faith and works which created the unity to push that baby through (the baby was the idea of the church).

There was always some type of fundraising going on. There was no kitchen in the storefront so there was rarely any dinner selling, but there were bake sales, raffles and baby contests. As a matter of fact, my baby brother was in the first baby contest that Greater Monumental had.

It wasn't based on which baby was the cutest baby. It was based on the baby who sold the most tickets. I believe my brother came in first or second place. I'm not sure which one. That little storefront church became a powerhouse of worship. It was the birthplace of many lifelong friendships and kinships for my brother and me, as well. Attending Sunday school with other children in our age range, six and seven, who had come to church with their parents and/or grandparents, enabled us, the children, to form a bond much like, and sometimes better, than family.

Although a few were older and some were younger, we considered one another as cousins. At first, the choir consisted of about four or five ladies, and at least three of them each considered themselves the lead singer, the director and the president. Eventually, Reverend had to intervene and assign duties. One became the director, one became the assistant director, and they each took turns as soloists. The pastor became the president for a while.

Before long, Selena and Reverend JA Williams were able to rent an organ and piano. With the musicians in place, the organist and pianist, the choir singing to the power of the Lord come down and Jay preaching his heart out, next thing we knew we had four more choir members.

That made the choir look fuller and it was two rows now, about three   sopranos, three altos and two tenors. Upon completion of his sermon, every Sunday, Jay would open the doors of the church and extend an invitation to those who would desire a relationship with God, and those who wanted to become a member of the church. More often than not, he would welcome someone or many ones in with Christian experience, by a letter or as candidates for baptism.

However, his ministry was expanding. As a congregation, they were filling up those tan wooden rental chairs.

Two things I will never forget; those wooden folding chairs and the hand fans that would always have a picture of Dr. Martin Luther King Jr. or a funeral home advertisement. Most of the time, it was the A. R. Leak Funeral home. Incidentally, Mr. Leak provided the white Limo for Selena and Jay's wedding, which was beautiful. Their slogan was pretty hard to forget as well: "It's Time Truth Speaks." It would be years before I understood what that meant... Scary.

At the same time, Reverend J. A. Williams was making a name for himself and Greater Monumental Missionary Baptist Church. Invites were coming from other churches and other pastors came to run their revival services, their anniversary services, and back then he would preach every night, Monday through Friday. Some were in the Chicago land area while others were spread out from different parts of Michigan, Mississippi and Tennessee.

The members of Greater Monumental conducted bake sales, teas and raffles as fund raising efforts. Reverend, Sister Williams, and their whole little congregation were on one accord, praying and striving together to find and purchase a new church location suitable for their growing church family/ congregation.

Will they do it? Can they do it? The real question could possibly be, will they even last long enough to continue their search for a new church together as a couple?

Epilogue

Although Reverend and Selena were married, they were yet still newlyweds. However, Reverend's fan base was increasing and some of the sisters were joining the church for what some may say were the wrong reasons, while others might say they were joining for other reasons. I'm certain most would agree that it was at the very least the wrong time. Instead of a relationship with The Lord Our God, some were hoping for a relationship with the pastor, and not on a spiritual level, but on a personal level, one which would not always include the entire flocks company.

One sister in particular felt she had what it took to win Reverend's personal attention above and beyond all others... Ms. Sister Berkley.

Sister Berkley was a seasoned senior citizen. A light- skinned short woman of few words who wore a light brown, like a number four (for all of my hair/color scholars) short wig. Ms. Berkley always wore a, (what they called back then,) little black pill box hat on top of it. For those of you who remember and some of you may have worn them; back in those days, the 60's and 70's for sure the wigs themselves were more like hats so it was like a hat on a hat because the wigs were so thick. I guess it was to serve a lot of different purposes; one a woman could be certain her head was completely covered and two, it would last her a good while. I must say some of the women I would see wearing wigs really abused the length of time one should wear the same wig.

Especially, back in the day when wigs were most made out of synthetic fiber. After a period of time, whatever solution the wig manufacturers would treat and seal the wigs with, would either be brushed out or simply deteriorate and fiber would attract fiber, causing the tips and or ends of the wigs turn into little balls and knots.

Another sure sign that a wig is too old is when the wig is trying to get away from you—that is, the wig is running backwards. In other words, when the wig is lifting from the back or from the nape of one's head, it's time to let it go...release it. Men, those who wore them, were guilty of that too. I know I am not the only who have seen this, on the street, in the church and in my grandmother's salon, after they have made up their mind to get a new hair weev just before asking one of us to throw that wig in the garbage. Ms. Berkley didn't wear her wigs as long as some others did. I do recall seeing her wig in the early stage of the roll up, but the next Sunday, she had on a new wig; like most women and I don't blame her, she didn't want her gray hair exposed at all.

The only time Ms. Berkley would remove her black hat was when she played the organ. Other than that, you would never see her without it publicly. Her black pillbox hat, black tweed coat, black patent leather purse, referred to as a woman's pocketbook back then, and her shiny long black 1965 Cadillac were the standard for Ms. Berkley. Though it was the early 70's, she kept her car clean and neat. It still looked good, but in a plain sort of way, like a funeral car. She rarely smiled, strictly business as she would march to the beat of her own drum with her pocketbook handle resting in the bend of her arm and her gloves, black too covering her pale pink hands.

Sister Berkley was giving donations left and right, Sunday after Sunday. Whatever the church and Reverend needed she was willing to help. One Sunday, she wrote a check large enough to buy the organ for Greater Monumental Missionary Baptist church. Reverend Williams thanked her from the pulpit, said a special prayer for her and offered her the position of minister of music. She did manage to crack a smile and nod; like I said she didn't talk much.

Selena, of course, as the First Lady of Greater Monumental expressed her appreciation with words of gratitude and a warm handshake, which was accompanied by her winning smile. The choir director, choir members, everyone thanked her for buying the organ by giving a round of applause and a hearty "amen."

Sister Berkley was at least twenty-five years older than Reverend Williams, but she looked thirty-five to forty years older than he did. That didn't matter to her at all. She seem to be from "the money talks and all else walks" club. She had the persona that the only thing old about her was her money and since it's still spendable age is not a factor. Sister Berkley began to display her attraction to Reverend and it became more and more apparent that her motives had shifted from doing good deeds to expecting a return of a different kind of favor. Sister Berkley's religion had changed, so to speak. Her practice was geared toward the Reverend, and not the Lord. She wanted the pastor to lay hands on her, but not for prayers. Every Sunday, Sister Berkley always needed a word with Reverend Williams after service. For a while, he accommodated her in his small office, but he was never alone. Sometimes, it would be his wife Selena, one of his trusted deacons or trustees.

That was okay with Sister Berkley for a while, but that began to irritate her and she expressed it.

On occasion, Selena would offer to give them a little privacy. The lady was old and very faithful to the church, in spite of Reverend telling her that his wife would pray for her and with her about whatever the situation was. But, that is a real fine line a pastor has to walk. He had to be careful. Some parishioners/ members do disclose things to their pastors that they would never speak of in front of anyone else. However, if I were a minister, male or female, I wouldn't meet with anyone totally alone. Someone I trusted would always be close by, right outside my door. It's too much disrespect, dissension, jealousy and desperation, which can arise from the situation.

One Sunday after church, the weekend of Memorial Day, Sister Berkley apparently fed up with the chaperoned meetings with Reverend, handed a sealed envelope to one of the trustees addressed to Reverend J. A. Williams. The trustee stood in shock that she walked away so swiftly, he was accustomed to her waiting to see Reverend every Sunday afternoon. After quickly recovering, he went the few steps into Rev's office and handed him the envelope. Rev. didn't open the letter immediately; he was meeting with a couple of other members. Later, when most of the members had left and his office was clear of everyone, except Selena, a trustee and deacon or two who normally waited to walk out with them, he opened the envelope.

There was a letter inside, requesting his presence at her home for a private meeting. Sister Berkley explained further in the letter that she understood that he could not control the privacy at the church, but she could control it in her home. She went further, promising there would not be any interruptions and she would be expecting his call to set it up. He laughed it off; they all did. They were thinking of her as a lonely older lady; no harm, no worries. Everyone gathered their belongings and prepared to leave and lock up the church.

Later that evening, they were relaxing at home. All of a sudden, they started receiving prank calls. Selena answered the first couple of calls and the person would just hang up when Jay would answer they would just hold the phone quietly. That was before caller id and star 69, therefore back then, the only other option was to take the phone off the hook. However, the phone lines were the same phone lines for Selena's House of Beauty, which was downstairs. There were two lines that were set up. When the first line was in use, it automatically switched to the second lines number so they had to leave one line off the hook, while leaving the other line on hold for the rest of the evening. After wondering a while, they both thought...*could it be Ms. Berkley?*

Although Selena's dad, Henry, had been deceased a few years, Selena continued her Memorial Day ritual. The ritual was always bitter sweet. She had always loved her father and she grieved for him. Like most adult children, she wished her parents could have grown old together. However Selena was very proud as she reflected back on her father's final years. Selena had moved her daddy, Henry into the apartment that she shared with her mother Mary and her son El. Selena learned that her mother was truly phenomenal on an entirely new level by the way Mary took care of Henry. Mary bathed him, cooked and fed him, she did whatever needed to be done. The only thing she didn't do was give Henry his diabetic shot; my young Uncle El did that every day. The three of them took care of Henry until he was admitted back into the County Hospital. It didn't matter if Selena worked until midnight, whenever she got off she would get in her car and head straight for the hospital; she would have to sneak up to Henry's room through the staircase but it was worth it to see his eyes light up when he saw her...she never missed a day until he passed.

She cleaned his grave, planting flowers and talking to him at least once a year, sometime more. This was her way of keeping her daddy informed of her life. She would talk to him about her children, her mother, if she had bought a new car, her business and how she was expanding by moving her salon into a larger place, which was her own building now.

This particular year, Jay accompanied her to her dad's gravesite and became part of the ritual.

While at the cemetery, Selena's mind drifted back to the night before. She was wondering was it Ms. Berkley or someone else. She began to ask Jay what he thought about the calls the night before. She studied his demeanor and body language as he answered.

She noticed Jay seemed quite comfortable and relaxed. While smiling, he asked her, "What are you thinking, Baby?" As he burst into laughter, he stated, "That ain't nobody but Ms. Berkley, mad because I didn't call her after she left that letter yesterday."

Still studying him, Selena smiled back at Jay while she continued placing the flowers around her dad's grave. He was being transparent. He didn't seem to be hiding anything.

After leaving the cemetery, they were invited to one of the deacon's home for dinner. It was a pleasure because Selena and Jay both loved the way his wife, Sister Pearl cooked, especially her greens. The day was coming to a close so they went home, got comfortable, and just before the both of them could get in their respective spots in front of the TV, they heard a car pull up.

At first, they didn't think much of it. It could have been one of the neighbor's; perhaps it was one of the Latee brothers' cars.

They were their next door neighbors who had wives and their own families. Willie J and Willie C. were owners of Latee's, another hair shop. They had a sister who worked with them, as well. Their business was popping, too. There was enough money for everybody. They were known for finger waves in their multiple salons and beauty culture schools.

Anyhow, the headlights from the car were on for a pretty good while. This was before cars had auto off light timers. Intrigued by the longevity of the lights, they both took a peep out of the window and saw that it was neither of the neighbor's cars. Though it was dark outside, the car looked familiar.

They each took a second glance and neither of them could believe their eyes when they realized where they knew the car from.

"Do you see who that is?" Selena said to Jay.

"I can't believe it! She has lost her mind!" he responded back to Selena.

They both continued to stare out at the car, watching and waiting for any sign of movement. As Selena turned to walk away from the window, Jay's whisper halted her.

"Wait, wait, Baby. She's getting out of the car!" Jay whispered.

Their windows were open in order to allow the fresh cool summer night breeze to come in.

"Wonder where she thinks she's going and what is that in her hand?" Selena questioned in a louder tone. With that, she pivoted on one foot. Selena turned and barreled down the hall towards the bedroom.

Jay, in shock, followed behind Selena and asked her in a slightly panicked voice, "What we going to do?" He watched Selena reach for her never-leave-home without it .38 revolver. He never left home without his .45 either, but he thought, at least he hoped, it wouldn't be necessary for that night.

Selena snapped, "This broad done came to my house and it looked like she had a gun in her hand and you questioning me?!"

"We couldn't see it that good; I don't believe she had no gun."

Oh, Lord, I know, Jay thought to himself. *If we ever needed the Lord, we sure do need him now.*

Will there be peace or police?

The saga continues....

Selena—the girl who came to Chicago

Selena and her mother, Mary.

Selena and her father, Henry.

Selena's son, Elmer, Jr. "El" was hard at work as a teen in the new shop.

Selena, Elmer Parker, and their two daughters.

Selena with Sammy, her first employee, stylist, Manager.

Selena's Madam C.J. Walker's Text Book.

Selena's first hot stove heated with kerosene

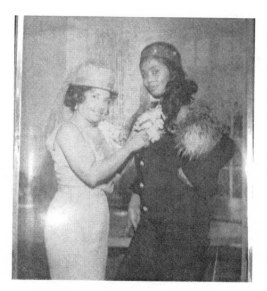

*The First Lady (inventor) of Hair Weev,
Christine Jenkins, with Selena.*

*Selena and Sarah
Vaughn.
Signed "To My
Favorite Beautician."*

Selena's Portraits

Selena's House of Beauty

First Lady Selena Williams and Reverend J.A. Williams

Selena's First Magazine Cover and Article: Beauty Trade

Mr. B. B. King, Selena, and I

Selena and her passion—hair.

Selena improved upon the original hair Weev machine by creating the E-Z Weev Machine, which is smaller and saves time.

Selena, my mentor, and I.

Selena chillaxing in her Chicago Loop location, on State Street that Great Street.

The Queen of Hair Weev, Selena, and The King of the Blues, B.B. King

About the Author

$\mathcal{B}$onnie Taylor-Williams, a twenty plus years cancer survivor, a professional third-generation Hair Weev Technician, a designer and instructor, grew up learning the family business of beauty and Hair Weev. Bonnie learned how to hair loom, (hand weft) human hair for weeving at the age of ten. By the age of fourteen, she was taught the art of Hair Weev technology. Because of her age and not yet being a licensed cosmetologist Bonnie was not allowed to practice Hair Weev professionally. After high School, Bonnie attended and completed Pivot Point International beauty school. Bonnie immediately began her professional career at Selena's House of Beauty & School of Hair Weev Technology's Chicago loop location. Some years later, while traveling from state to state teaching and exhibiting in many tradeshows and expos, Bonnie had her own products, "E-Z Beautee Extraordinary Detangling Maintenance System" developed for the care of commercial and one's own natural hair under her own company Beautee Inc. After appearing in several trade magazines (ShopTalk, Salon Profiles, and Elite), Bonnie was also included in the twenty-sixth edition of "Who's Who in the Midwest."

Bonnie, still wanting to write, attended various classes, some at Columbia College and Kennedy King and participated in the Universal Foundation for Better Living writer's group until becoming a foster parent. After decades in the hair industry, Bonnie enlarged her territory by following her mother, Juanita Dunbar, into the transportation business; becoming a second generation School bus owner/operator as a subcontractor for Dunbar Transportation, Inc.

She is now doing what she has longed to do...sharing her stories through writing.

Bonnie Taylor-Williams
www.bonnietaylorwilliams.com

CPSIA information can be obtained at www.ICGtesting.com
Printed in the USA
LVOW10s0825140616

492346LV00001B/53/P